LUXURIOUS
LACE
BY KNIT PICKS

Photography by Amy Cave

Printed in the United States of America

First Printing, 2017

ISBN 978-1-62767-164-4

Versa Press, Inc
800-447-7829

www.versapress.com

CONTENTS

LEAF OUT SHAWL

by Tetiana Otruta

FINISHED MEASUREMENTS

56.25 (72.5)"wingspan, 22 (26.5)" deep, relaxed after blocking

YARN

Knit Picks Capretta (80% Fine Merino Wool, 10% Cashmere, 10% Nylon; 230 yards/50g): Hunter 25599, 3 (4) balls

NEEDLES

US 6 (4 mm) 32" or longer circular needle, or size to obtain gauge
US 5 (3.75 mm) 32" or longer circular needle, or one size smaller than size to obtain gauge

NOTIONS

Stitch Markers
Yarn Needle

GAUGE

18 sts and 26 rows = 4" in St st with larger needle, blocked.
7.5" width of Lace Edge Chart A with smaller needle, blocked; measurement is taken over the first 2 garter st rows

Leaf Out Shawl

Notes:

Leaf Out Shawl is a half circle shawl worked from center back to bottom edge. The lace edge is worked sideways with short row shaping, joining to the shawl body as you go.

If using Chart A, read RS rows from right to left and WS rows from left to right.

Cable Cast-On: *Insert RH needle between the first two stitches on LH needle, wrap yarn around needle and bring through. Transfer the newly created stitch onto LH needle; rep from * until you have cast on the specified number of sts.

Joining Stitch: The lace edge is worked sideways and attached as you go to the shawl body. Joining is worked by SKP in RS row which joins the last lace edge stitch to the next live body stitch. This joining stitch is slipped WYIF in the next WS row.

BO K-wise: K1, *K1, pull the first st on the RH needle over the second st and off the right needle; rep from * to end.

W&T: WYIF, slip the next st P-wise from LH needle to RH. Bring the yarn to the back between the needles. Slip the stitch from RH needle back to LH needle. Turn the work so WS is facing you, ready to knit.
In the next RS row pick up the wrap with RH needle from back to front. Place the wrap onto LH needle, over and behind the stitch it was wrapping. Purl together the wrap and the stitch that is wrapped.

DIRECTIONS

Setup Rows
With larger needle, CO 3 sts.
Row 1 (RS): K3.
Row 2 (WS): K1, M1, K1, M1, K1. 5 sts.
Row 3: K2, M1, K1, M1, K2. 7 sts.
Row 4: K7.
Row 5: K2, YO, K1, PM, YO, KFB, YO, PM, K1, YO, K2. 12 sts.
Row 6: K2, P8, K2.
Row 7: K2, YO, K2, SM, YO, K2, YO, K2, YO, SM, K2, YO, K2. 17 sts.
Row 8: K2, P13, K2.
Row 9: K2, YO, K3, SM, YO, K3, PM, YO, K2TOG, K2, YO, SM, K3, YO, K2. 21 sts.
Row 10: K2, P17, K2.

Shawl Body
Rows 1, 3, and 5 (RS): K2, YO, K to M, SM, YO, K to M, SM, YO, K2TOG, K to M, YO, SM, K to last 2 sts, YO, K2. 4 sts inc.
Row 2 and all WS Rows: K2, P to 2 sts from end, K2.
Row 7: K2, YO, K3, YO, K2TOG, K2, SM, YO, K3, YO, K2TOG, K2, SM, YO, K2TOG, K1, SKP, YO, K3, YO, SM, K2, SKP, YO, K3, YO, K2. 4 sts inc. 37 sts
Rows 9 and 11: K2, YO, K to M, SM, YO, K to M, SM, YO, K2TOG, K to M, YO, SM, K to 2 sts from end, YO, K2. 4 sts inc.
Row 13: K2, YO, K3, YO, K2TOG, K5, SM, YO, K3, YO, K2TOG, K5, SM, YO, K2TOG, K4, SKP, YO, K3, YO, SM, K5, SKP, YO, K3, YO, K2. 4 sts inc. 49 sts
Rows 15, 17, 21, and 23: K2, YO, K to M, SM, YO, K to M, SM, YO, K2TOG, K to M, YO, SM, K to 2 sts from end, YO, K2. 4 sts inc.
Row 19: K2, YO, K3, YO, K2TOG, [K4, YO, K2TOG] rep to 2 sts from M, K2, SM, YO, K3, YO, K2TOG, [K4, YO, K2TOG] rep to 2 sts from M, K2, SM, YO, K2TOG, K1, SKP, YO, [K4, SKP, YO] rep to 3 sts from M, K3, YO, SM, K2, SKP, YO, [K4, SKP, YO] rep to 5 sts from end, K3, YO, K2. 4 sts inc.
Row 25: K2, YO, K3, YO, K2TOG, [K4, YO, K2TOG] rep to 5 sts from M, K5, SM, YO, K3, YO, K2TOG, [K4, YO, K2TOG] rep to 5 sts from M, K5, SM, YO, K2TOG, K4, SKP, YO, [K4, SKP, YO] rep to 3 sts from M, K3, YO, SM, K5, SKP, YO, [K4, SKP, YO] rep to 5 sts from end, K3, YO, K2. 4 sts inc.

Rep Rows 15-26 five (eight) times more. 193 (265) sts.

Work Rows 15-22 (15-16) once more, ending with WS row. 209 (269) sts. Do not cut yarn.

Chart A Lace Edge
Using Cable Cast-On, CO 32 sts on LH needle.
Rows 1 (RS): K31, SKP (joining st).
Row 2 (WS): Sl1 WYIF, K to end.

Switch to smaller needle. For all RS rows, the last SKP is a joining st.

Row 1 (RS): Sl1 WYIF, K1, YO, K2, PM, K2, YO, SKP, P2, YO, K2TOG, K3TOG, [YO, K1] 3 times, YO, SSKP, SKP, YO, P2, K2, YO, SKP, P2, SKP.
Row 2 (WS): Sl1 WYIF, K2, P2, YO, P2TOG, K2, P13, K2, P2, YO, P2TOG, SM, K2, P1, K2.
Row 3: Sl1 WYIF, [K1, YO] twice, K2, SM, K2, YO, SKP, P2, YO, K3TOG, YO, K7, YO, SSKP, YO, P2, K2, YO, SKP, P2, SKP.
Row 4: Sl1 WYIF, K2, P2, YO, P2TOG, K2, P13, K2, P2, YO, P2TOG, SM, K2, P3, K2.
Row 5: Sl1 WYIF, K1, YO, K3, YO, K2, SM, K2, YO, SKP, P2, YO, K2TOG, YO, K1, YO, K2, S2KP, K2, YO, K1, YO, SKP, YO, P1, W&T.
Row 6: K1, P15, K2, P2, YO, P2TOG, SM, K2, P5, K2.
Row 7: Sl1 WYIF, SKP, YO, S2KP, YO, K2TOG, K1, SM, K2, YO, SKP, P2, YO, K2TOG, YO, K3, K1, S2KP, K1, YO, K3, YO, SKP, YO, P2, K2, YO, SKP, P2, SKP.
Row 8: Sl1 WYIF, K2, P2, YO, P2TOG, K2, P17, K2, P2, YO, P2TOG, SM, K7.
Row 9: BO 3 sts K-wise, K1, YO, K2, SM, K2, YO, SKP, P2, YO, K2TOG twice, K3, YO, S2KP, YO, K3, SKP twice, YO, P2, K2, YO, SKP, P2, SKP.
Row 10: Sl1 WYIF, K2, P2, YO, P2TOG, K2, P15, K2, P2, YO, P2TOG, SM, K2, P1, K2.
Row 11: Sl1 WYIF, [K1, YO] twice, K2, SM, K2, YO, SKP, P2, YO, K2TOG 3 times, [K1, YO] twice, K1, SKP 3 times, YO, P2, K2, YO, SKP, P2, SKP.
Row 12: Sl1 WYIF K2, P2, YO, P2TOG, K2, P13, K2, P2, YO, P2TOG, SM, K2, P3, K2.
Row 13: Sl1 WYIF, K1, YO, K3, YO, K2, SM, K2, YO, SKP, P2, YO, K2TOG, K3TOG, [YO, K1] 3 times, YO, SSKP, SKP, YO, P2, K2, YO, SKP, P2, SKP.
Row 14: Sl1 WYIF, K2, P2, YO, P2TOG, K2, P13, K2, P2, YO, P2TOG, SM, K2, P5, K2.
Row 15: Sl1 WYIF, SKP, YO, S2KP, YO, K2TOG, K1, SM, K2, YO, SKP, P2, YO, K3TOG, YO, K7, YO, SSKP, YO, P2, K2, YO, SKP, P2, SKP.

Row 16: Sl1 WYIF, K2, P2, YO, P2TOG, K2, P13, K2, P2, YO, P2TOG, SM, K7.

Row 17: BO 3 sts K-wise, K1, YO, K2, SM, K2, YO, SKP, P2, YO, K2TOG, YO, K1, YO, K2, S2KP, K2, YO, K1, YO, SKP, YO, P1, W&T.

Row 18: K1, P15, K2, P2, YO, P2TOG, SM, K2, P1, K2.

Row 19: Sl1 WYIF, [K1, YO] twice, K2, SM, K2, YO, SKP, P2, YO, K2TOG, YO, K3, YO, K1, S2KP, K1, YO, K3, YO, SKP, YO, P2, K2, YO, SKP, P2, SKP.

Row 20: Sl1 WYIF, K2, P2, YO, P2TOG, K2, P17, K2, P2, YO, P2TOG, SM, K2, P3, K2.

Row 21: Sl1 WYIF, K1, YO, K3, YO, K2, SM, K2, YO, SKP, P2, YO, K2TOG twice, K3, YO, S2KP, YO, K3, SKP twice, YO, P2, K2, YO, SKP, P2, SKP.

Row 22: Sl1 WYIF, K2, P2, YO, P2TOG, K2, P15, K2, P2, YO, P2TOG, SM, K2, P5, K2.

Row 23: Sl1 WYIF, SKP, YO, S2KP, YO, K2TOG, K1, SM, K2, YO, SKP, P2, YO, K2TOG 3 times, [K1, YO] twice, K1, SKP 3 times, YO, P2, K2, YO, SKP, P2, SKP.

Row 24: Sl1 WYIF, K2, P2, YO, P2TOG, K2, P13, K2, P2, YO, P2TOG, SM, K7.

Row 25: BO 3 sts K-wise, K1, YO, K2, SM, K2, YO, SKP, P2, YO, K2TOG, K3TOG, [YO, K1] 3 times, YO, SSKP, SKP, YO, P2, K2, YO, SKP, P2, SKP.

Row 26: Sl1 WYIF, K2, P2, YO, P2TOG, K2, P13, K2, P2, YO, P2TOG, SM, K2, P1, K2.

Rep Rows 3-26 until all shawl body sts have been joined except the last one st.

Note: The last pattern rep ends with Row 15.

Next Row (WS): Sl1 WYIF, K to end.

Switch to larger needle.

Row 1 (RS): BO 7 sts K-wise, K to 1 st from end of lace edge section, SKP (joining st).

BO row (WS): Sl1 WYIF, *K1, pull the first st on the RH needle over the second st and off the right needle; rep from * to end.

Finishing

Weave in yarn ends; trim after blocking. Soak shawl in lukewarm water (with soap for fiber if desired) for 10-15 minutes. Rinse and roll in towel to get rid of excess water. Pin out on a clean sheet or blocking board. Let dry and unpin only when dry, then trim yarn tails.

Chart A

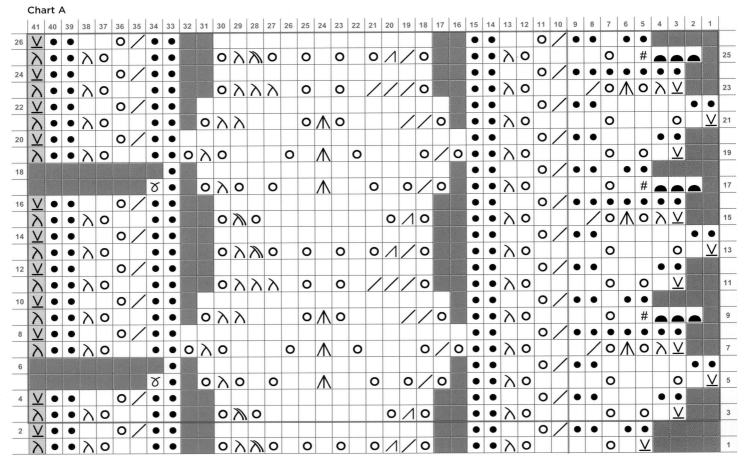

Legend

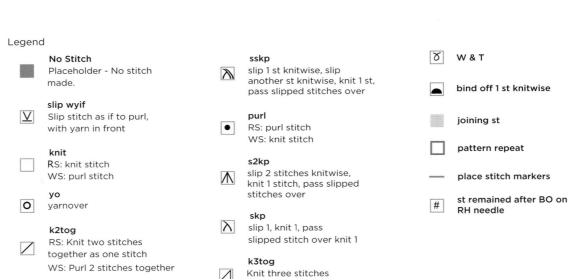

No Stitch
Placeholder - No stitch made.

slip wyif
Slip stitch as if to purl, with yarn in front

knit
RS: knit stitch
WS: purl stitch

yo
yarnover

k2tog
RS: Knit two stitches together as one stitch
WS: Purl 2 stitches together

sskp
slip 1 st knitwise, slip another st knitwise, knit 1 st, pass slipped stitches over

purl
RS: purl stitch
WS: knit stitch

s2kp
slip 2 stitches knitwise, knit 1 stitch, pass slipped stitches over

skp
slip 1, knit 1, pass slipped stitch over knit 1

k3tog
Knit three stitches together as one

W & T

bind off 1 st knitwise

joining st

pattern repeat

place stitch markers

 # st remained after BO on RH needle

FUCHSIA CRESCENT SHAWL

by Renate Siebke

FINISHED MEASUREMENTS

S (M, L): 19 (21.25, 23.5)" tall x 56 (63, 70)" wide across top edge. Sample shown in Size L

YARN

Knit Picks Palette (100% Peruvian Highland Wool; 231 yards/50g): Lingonberry Heather 25998, 3 (4, 4) balls

NEEDLES

US 5 (3.75mm) 24" or longer circular needles, or size to obtain gauge
US 7 (4.5mm) 24" or longer circular needles, or 2 sizes larger than size to obtain gauge

NOTIONS

Yarn Needle
Locking Stitch Markers, safety-pins or waste yarn to secure live center stitches
Scissors

GAUGE

18 sts and 30 rows = 4" in St st on smaller needles, blocked.
Each module is 7" wide x 4.5" high, blocked. (Gauge for this project is approximate)

Fuchsia Crescent Shawl

Notes:

Fuchsia Crescent Shawl is an easily knit crescent-shaped symmetrical shawl, that is sure to become your favorite accessory for almost any occasion! Modules are worked in lace knitting, mainly using K, P, YO, SSK, K2tog, SK2P and CDD sts. An elastic CO method is used to make the bottom edge stretchy and uniform. At first glance, the Fuchsia Crescent is a seemingly complicated shawl, but once the first 3 or 4 modules are finished, you will only need to look at the written instructions or charts for a few RS rows and one WS row.

The top edge has a slim eyelet finish, which matches the CO edge, allowing the shawl to be blocked into a uniquely curved triangle. By combining the simplicity of basic stitches with an unusual and intriguing construction, the Fuchsia Crescent creates a feminine shawl that looks at its best in fingering weight yarn.

This pattern contains fully written instructions and options for 2 slightly more shallow versions as well 3 size options with 7 (8, 9) rows of full modules. This shawl can be enlarged even further by adding more rows.

Elastic Cast-On:
Using larger needles and Jeny's Surprisingly Stretchy Cast-On, make a slip knot and place it on the right-hand needle by pulling the working yarn through the loop. Make sure the knot is at the end of the yarn, not on the working-yarn side. Make another slipknot next to the first one, then continue making slipknots until the required number of stitches are CO. Practice this technique with a short strand of scrap yarn, to get the tension right and ensure an even distance between cast-on-stitches.
If you find this method too fiddly you can use the Knitted CO:
http://tutorials.knitpicks.com/wptutorials/knitted-cast-on/

Elastic Bind Off: K1, *K1, Sl the two sts on your right needle back to left needle and K2tog TBL; rep from * until all sts are BO.

Special Stitches
A Stitch: PU 1 st from center st of module below.
B Stitch: PU 1 st from Sl st edge of module of previous row of modules.
C Stitch: K into st 2 rows below next st on left needle, YO then K into same st, let unknit st on left needle drop off needle. 2 sts inc.

Read the charts RS rows (odd numbers) from right to left, and WS rows (even numbers) from left to right.

Do not cut yarn unless stated. Place the last stitch of each module on a locking marker, if you do not continue with the next module right away.

The shawl begins with the bottom center module, Module 1. Then the Left Side Full Modules are knit, followed by the Right Side Full Modules. The center is filled in with Center Full Modules. After all the Full Modules are done, the top line of Half Modules is knit: left, right and center. The shawl is finished with an eyelet border across the top.

Left Side: Starting at the bottom, the Left Side Full Modules 3, 6,

10, 15, 21 and 28 are all worked the same way. Then the Left Side Half Module 36 is knit, placing the 7 live stitches remaining on a locking marker.

Right Side: Starting at the bottom again, the Right Side Full Modules 2, 4, 7, 11, 16, and 22 are all worked the same way. Then the Right Side Half Module 29 is knit. It is best to use a new ball of yarn for Modules 2 and 4. Leftover balls can be used for the later right side modules.

Center: Work a Center Full Module in the gap between Modules 2 and 3. All remaining Center Full Modules are worked in the same way. Follow the schematic and work Center Half Modules to finish the top row of modules. You will not need to cut the yarn until you finish the Half Modules.

For each Full Module, you will work the appropriate Module Row 1 and then work Full Module Chart Rows 2-33. Similarly, for each Half Module you will work the appropriate Half Module Row 1 and then work Half Module Chart Rows 2-19.

The Schematic shows the Module numbers for size Small. Medium and Large are not pictured, but can be worked as follows:
Small: Modules 1-28 are full modules and Modules 29 - 36 are half modules.
Medium: Modules 1-36 are full modules and Modules 37 - 45 are half modules.
Large: Modules 1-45 are full modules and Modules 46 - 55 are half modules.

If you want to achieve a shallower shawl with a wider wingspan, you may skip the first module or even the first 3 modules. In this case, you will start off 2 or 3 of your lines of modules with Setup Row 1. Those modules are detached and will be joined to the left and right in the next row of modules.

DIRECTIONS

Module 1
Chart Setup Row 1 (RS): With larger needle, CO 34.

Work Full Module Chart Rows 2-33 once. The Full Module Chart Rows 2-33 instructions are both charted and written.

Full Module Chart Rows 2-33
Row 2 (WS): With larger needle, Sl 1 WYIF, K33. 34 sts.
Row 3 (RS): Sl 1 WYIF, K33.
Row 4: Sl 1 WYIF, P, *YO, K2tog; rep from * to last 2 sts, YO, P, K. 1 st inc. 35 sts.
Row 5: Sl 1 WYIF, K34.
Row 6: Sl 1 WYIF, K34.
Row 7: Sl 1 WYIF, K34.
Row 8: Sl 1 WYIF, P to last st, K1.

Change to smaller needle.
Row 9: Sl 1 WYIF, K34.
Rows 10 and 12: Sl 1 WYIF, P to last st, K1.
Row 11: Sl 1 WYIF, K34.
Row 13: Sl 1 WYIF, K4, SSK, K8, K2tog, YO, K into st 2 rows below next st on left needle, YO then K into same st, let unknit st on left needle drop off needle, YO, SSK, K8, K2tog, K5.
Row 14: Sl 1 WYIF, P12, SSP, P5, P2tog, P12, K1. 2 sts dec. 33 sts.

Row 15: Sl 1 WYIF, K4, SSK, K5, (K2tog, YO) twice, K1, (YO, SSK) twice, K5, K2tog, K5. 2 sts dec. 31 sts.
Row 16 and all WS rows through Row 32: Sl 1 WYIF, P to 1 st before end, K1.
Row 17: Sl 1 WYIF, K4, YO, SSK twice, K1, (K2tog, YO) twice, K3, (YO, SSK) twice, K1, K2tog twice, YO, K5. 2 sts dec. 29 sts.
Row 19: Sl 1 WYIF, K3, SSK, YO, SSK, K2tog, (YO, CDD) 3 times, YO, SSK, K2tog, YO, K2tog, K4. 6 sts dec. 23 sts.
Row 21: Sl 1 WYIF, K2, CDD, YO, SSK, CDD, YO, K1, YO, CDD, K2tog, YO, CDD, K3. 6 sts dec. 17 sts.
Row 23: Sl 1 WYIF, K2, SSK, YO, SSK, CDD, K2tog, YO, K2tog, K3. 4 sts dec. 13 sts.
Row 25: Sl 1 WYIF, K2, SSK, SK2P, K2tog, K3. 4 sts dec. 9 sts.
Row 27: Sl 1 WYIF, K2, SK2P, K3. 2 sts dec. 7 sts.
Row 29: Sl 1 WYIF, K1, CDD, K2. 2 sts dec. 5 sts.
Row 31: Sl 1 WYIF, CDD, K1. 2 sts dec. 3 sts.
Row 33: CDD. 2 sts dec. Place live stitch on locking marker. 1 st.

For Modules 2, 4 and all Right Side Full Modules
Right Module Chart
Row 1: With larger needle, CO 17, (PU 1 st from Sl st edge of module of previous row of modules) 17 times. 34 sts.

Work Full Module Chart Rows 2-33 once.

For Modules 5, 8 and all Center Full Modules
Center Module Chart
Row 1: With larger needle, PU 1 st from center st of module below, (PU 1 st from Sl st edge of module of previous row of modules) 33 times. 34 sts.

Work Full Module Chart Rows 2-33 once.

For Modules 3, 6 and all Left Side Full Modules
Left Module Chart
Row 1: With larger needle, PU 1 st from center st of module below, (PU 1 st from Sl st edge of module of previous row of modules) 16 times, CO 17. 34 sts.

Work Full Module Chart Rows 2-33 once.

Half Modules
With larger needle, work appropriate Row 1 instructions, same as for the Full Modules and then work Half Module Chart Rows 2-19 once.

Half Module Chart Rows 2-19
Row 2 (WS): Sl 1 WYIF, K33. 34 sts.
Row 3 (RS): Sl 1 WYIF, K33.
Row 4: Sl 1 WYIF, K2tog, *YO, K2tog; rep from * to last st, K1. 33 sts.
Row 5: Sl 1 WYIF, K32.
Row 6: Sl 1 WYIF, K1, K2tog, K25, K2tog, K2. 31 sts.
Row 7: Sl 1 WYIF, K30.
Row 8: Sl 1, P to 1 st before end, K1.

Change to smaller needle.

Row 9: Sl 1 WYIF, K1, SSK, K8, K2tog, YO, SK2P, YO, SSK, K8, K2tog, K2. 4 sts dec. 27 sts.
Row 10 and all WS rows through Row 18: Sl 1, P to 1 st before end, K1.

Row 11: Sl 1 WYIF, K1, SSK, YO, SSK, K2, SSK, K2tog, YO, K3, YO, SSK, K2tog, K2, K2tog, YO, K2tog, K2. 4 sts dec. 23 sts.
Row 13: Sl 1 WYIF, K1, SSK, YO, SSK, K2, SSK, YO, CDD, YO, K2tog, K2, K2tog, YO, K2tog, K2. 4 sts dec. 19 sts.
Row 15: Sl 1 WYIF, K1, SSK, YO, SSK, K2, CDD, K2, K2tog, YO, K2tog, K2. 4 sts dec. 15 sts.
Row 17: Sl 1 WYIF, K1, SSK, YO, SSK, CDD, K2tog, YO, K2tog, K2. 4 sts dec. 11 sts.
Row 19: Sl 1 WYIF, K1, SSK, CDD, K2tog, K2. Secure these 7 sts using a locking marker. These sts will be worked for the eyelet-border. Cut yarn, leaving a short tail to weave in.

Eyelet Border
With smaller needles, work Rows 1-6 of the Border Chart once. You will also be working the center stitch of the last row of Full Modules between Half Modules, which have been worked before at the start of the Half modules as well as working the 7 live stitches from the locking marker. You can weave in the tails of yarn from the Half Modules when you come across them.

Border Chart (worked flat over multiple of 24 sts)
Row 1 (RS): CO 1, (PU 1 st from Sl st edge of module of previous row of modules) 9 times, K2, *CDD, K2, (PU 1 st from Sl st edge of module of previous row of modules) 9 times, PU 1 st from center st of module below, (PU 1 st from Sl st edge of module of previous row of modules) 9 times, K2; rep from * to the center of the last Half Module, CDD, K2, (PU 1 st from Sl st edge of module of previous row of modules) 8 times, CO 1. (Total number of sts should be a multiple of 24 sts, but if you are off a little it will be fine as long as you have a multiple of 2 plus 4 or 5 sts.)
Row 2 (WS): K.
Row 3: K.
Row 4: K1, P1, *YO, K2tog, rep from * to last 2 sts, YO, P1, K1, (or rep from * to last 3 sts, YO, P1, YO, P1, K1).
Row 5: K.
Row 6: K.

BO using Elastic BO.

Finishing:
Weave in ends, wash and block hard according to Schematic, make sure to pin out each eyelet separately.

Set Up Chart Row 1

35	34	33	32	31	30	29	28	27	26	25	24	23	22	21	20	19	18	17	16	15	14	13	12	11	10	9	8	7	6	5	4	3	2	1
▨	ᘓ	ᘓ	ᘓ	ᘓ	ᘓ	ᘓ	ᘓ	ᘓ	ᘓ	ᘓ	ᘓ	ᘓ	ᘓ	ᘓ	ᘓ	ᘓ	ᘓ	ᘓ	ᘓ	ᘓ	ᘓ	ᘓ	ᘓ	ᘓ	ᘓ	ᘓ	ᘓ	ᘓ	ᘓ	ᘓ	ᘓ	ᘓ	ᘓ	ᘓ	1

Center Module Row 1

35	34	33	32	31	30	29	28	27	26	25	24	23	22	21	20	19	18	17	16	15	14	13	12	11	10	9	8	7	6	5	4	3	2	1
▨	△	△	△	△	△	△	△	△	△	△	△	△	△	△	△	△	△	△	△	△	△	△	△	△	△	△	△	△	△	△	△	△	△	+	1

Right Module Row 1

33	32	31	30	29	28	27	26	25	24	23	22	21	20	19	18	17	16	15	14	13	12	11	10	9	8	7	6	5	4	3	2	1
▨	△	△	△	△	△	△	△	△	△	△	△	△	△	△	△	ᘓ	ᘓ	ᘓ	ᘓ	ᘓ	ᘓ	ᘓ	ᘓ	ᘓ	ᘓ	ᘓ	ᘓ	ᘓ	ᘓ	ᘓ	ᘓ	1

Left Module Row 1

35	34	33	32	31	30	29	28	27	26	25	24	23	22	21	20	19	18	17	16	15	14	13	12	11	10	9	8	7	6	5	4	3	2	1
▨	ᘓ	ᘓ	ᘓ	ᘓ	ᘓ	ᘓ	ᘓ	ᘓ	ᘓ	ᘓ	ᘓ	ᘓ	ᘓ	ᘓ	ᘓ	ᘓ	ᘓ	△	△	△	△	△	△	△	△	△	△	△	△	△	△	△	△	+	1

Legend

purl
RS: purl stitch
WS: knit stitch

slip
RS: Slip stitch as if to purl, holding yarn in back
WS: Slip stitch as if to purl, holding yarn in front

knit
RS: knit stitch
WS: purl stitch

p2tog
RS: Purl 2 stitches together
WS: Knit 2 stitches together

yo
yarn over

No Stitch
Placeholder - No stitch made.

sl1 k2tog psso
slip 1, k2tog, pass slip stitch over k2tog

ssk
RS: Slip one stitch as if to knit, slip another stitch as if to knit. Insert left-hand needle into front of these 2 stitches and knit them together
WS: Purl two stitches together in back loops, inserting needle from the left, behind and into the backs of the 2nd & 1st stitches in that order

k2tog
RS: Knit two stitches together as one stitch
WS: Purl 2 stitches together

Central Double Dec
RS: Slip first and second stitches together as if to knit. Knit 1 stitch. Pass two slipped stitches over the knit stitch.
WS: Slip first and second stitches together as it to purl through the back loop. Purl 1 stitch. Pass two slipped stitches over the purl stitch.

A stitch
pick up one stitch from center stitch of module below

cast on
cast on one stitch

B stitch
pick up one stitch from slip stitch edge of module of previous row of tiers

C Stitch
Knit into st 2 rows below next stitch on left needle, YO then K into same stitch, let unknit stitch on left needle drop off needle. 2 sts inc

pattern repeat

Module Layout

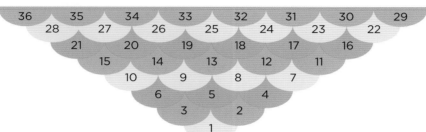

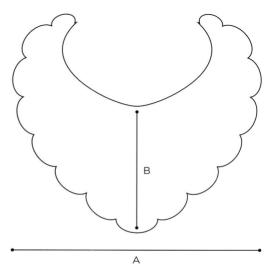

A 59"
B 22"

Half Module Chart Rows 2-19

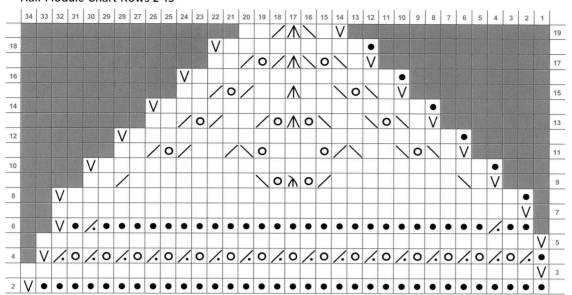

Full Module Chart Rows 2-33

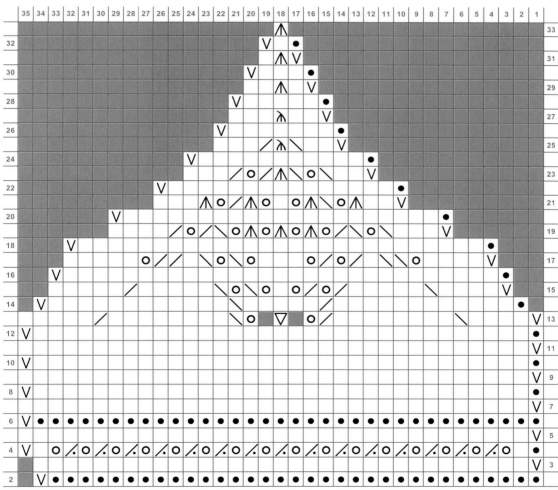

Border Chart

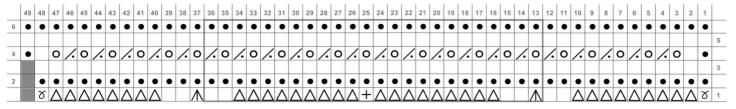

GERALDINE

by Mone Dräger

FINISHED MEASUREMENTS
68" wide along top edge x 26" high

YARN
Knit Picks Alpaca Cloud Lace Yarn (100% Baby Alpaca, 440 yards/50g): Hugh 26770, 2 hanks

NEEDLES
US 5 (3.25mm) 32" or longer circular needle, or size to obtain gauge

NOTIONS
Yarn Needle
Stitch Markers
Fine Crochet Hook
1,263 beads, size 6/0, #81611 clear with silver lining

GAUGE
24 sts and 40 rows = 4" over St st, blocked.
24 sts and 26 rows = 4" in Geraldine Charts A and B lace pattern, blocked. Gauge is not crucial for the project, but will affect yardage needed and finished size

Geraldine Shawl

Notes:

This semi-circle shaped shawl is knit from the top down. The sections in stockinette stitch alternate with sections in a traditional Shetland lace pattern. To establish the pattern, increases are made in the Stockinette section with the first lace insertion. All following increases are made in the set-up row of the lace stripes, then stitches are increased before working the knit-on border.

The lace pattern stays the same throughout the shawl body, but it increases in size. The lace starts as a small insertion in the Stockinette section and then becoming lace stripes that grow wider towards the bottom. Work as many rows as indicated, repeating Rows 1-4 of Chart B as necessary. All lace stripes end with a right side row, Row 3 of the chart. To embellish the lace pattern, small beads are added with a fine crochet hook. The border is knit sideways on to the main part. It picks up the motifs of the lace pattern and is also beaded.

Geraldine Chart A (worked flat over 13 sts)
Row 1 (WS): P4, P2tog TBL, YO, P1, YO, P2tog, P4.
Row 2 (RS): K3, K2tog, YO, K3, YO, SSK, K3.
Row 3: P1, P2tog TBL, YO, P1, YO, P2tog, B&P, P2tog TBL, YO, P1, YO, P2tog, P1.
Row 4: K2tog, YO, K3, YO, Sk2p, YO, K3, YO, SSK.
Row 5: (P1, YO, P2tog, B&P, P2tog TBL, YO) twice, P1.
Row 6: K2, YO, Sk2p, YO, K3, YO, Sk2p, YO, K2.
Row 7: P4, YO, P2tog, B&P, P2tog TBL, YO, P4.
Row 8: K5, YO, Sk2p, YO, K5.

Geraldine Chart B (worked flat over a multiple of 6 sts plus 7 sts)
Row 1 (RS): K2tog, *YO, K3, YO, Sk2p; rep from * to last 6 sts, YO, K3, YO, SSK.
Row 2 (WS): *P1, YO, P2tog, B&P, P2tog TBL, YO; rep from * to last st, P1.
Row 3: K1, *K1, YO, Sk2p, YO, K2; rep from * to end.
Row 4: P1, P2tog TBL, YO, P1, YO, P2tog, *B&P, P2tog TBL, YO, P1, YO, P2tog; rep from * to last st, P1.
Rep Rows 1-4 for pattern.

Geraldine Border Chart (worked flat)
Row 1 (RS): K1, SSK, YO, SSK, K2tog, YO, K1, K2tog, YO twice, SSK, K2tog, YO, K7, SKP (using one border and one 'body' st). 21 sts.
Row 2 (WS): Sl1 WYIF, P8, YO, P2tog, P1, K1, P3, YO, P2tog, P1, YO, P2. 22 sts.
Row 3: K2, (YO, K1, K2tog) twice, YO twice, SSK, K2tog, YO, K9, SKP (using one border and one 'body' st). 23 sts.
Row 4: Sl1 WYIF, P10, YO, P2tog, P1, K1, P3, YO, P2tog, P1, YO, P2. 24 border sts.
Row 5: K2, (YO, K1, K2tog) twice, YO twice, SSK, K2tog, YO, K11, SKP (using one border and one 'body' st). 25 sts.
Row 6: Sl1 WYIF, P2, P2tog TBL, YO, P1, YO, P2tog, P5, YO, P2tog, P1, K1, P3, YO, P2tog, P1, YO, P2. 26 sts.
Row 7: K2, (YO, K1, K2tog) twice, YO twice, SSK, K2tog, YO, K5, K2tog, YO, K3, YO, SSK, K1, SKP (using one border and one 'body' st). 27 sts.

Row 8: Sl1 WYIF, P2, YO, P2tog, B&P, P2tog TBL, YO, P1, YO, P2tog, P4, YO, P2tog, P1, K1, P3, YO, P2tog, P1, YO, P2. 28 sts.
Row 9: K2, (YO, K1, K2tog) twice, YO twice, SSK, K2tog, YO, K4, K2tog, YO, K3, YO, Sk2p, YO, K3, SKP (using one border and one 'body' st). 29 sts.
Row 10: Sl1 WYIF, P2, P2tog TBL, YO, P1, YO, P2tog, B&P, P2tog TBL, YO, P1, YO, P2tog, P3, YO, P2tog, P1, K1, P3, YO, P2tog, P1, YO, P2. 30 sts.
Row 11: K2, (YO, K1, K2tog) twice, YO twice, SSK, (K2tog, YO, K3) twice, YO, Sk2p, YO, K3, YO, SSK, K1, SKP (using one border and one 'body' st). 31 sts.
Row 12: Sl1 WYIF, P2, (YO, P2tog, B&P, P2tog TBL, YO, P1) twice, P1, P2tog TBL, YO, P4, K1, P2tog TBL, YO, P1, P2tog TBL, YO, P2tog TBL, P1. 30 sts.
Row 13: K1, SSK, YO, SSK, K1, YO, SSK, K2tog, YO twice, SSK, K1, YO, SSK, K2, (YO, Sk2p, YO, K3) twice, SKP (using one border and one 'body' st). 29 sts.
Row 14: Sl1 WYIF, P2, P2tog TBL, YO, P1, YO, P2tog, B&P, P2tog TBL, YO, P3, P2tog TBL, YO, P4, K1, P2tog TBL, YO, P1, P2tog TBL, YO, P2tog TBL, P1. 28 sts.
Row 15: K1, SSK, YO, SSK, K1, YO, SSK, K2tog, YO twice, SSK, K1, YO, SSK, K3, YO, Sk2p, YO, K3, YO, SSK, K1, SKP (using one border and one 'body' st). 27 sts.
Row 16: Sl1 WYIF, P2, YO, P2tog, B&P, (P2tog TBL, YO, P4) twice, K1, P2tog TBL, YO, P1, P2tog TBL, YO, P2tog TBL, P1. 26 sts.
Row 17: K1, SSK, YO, SSK, K1, YO, SSK, K2tog, YO twice, SSK, K1, YO, SSK, K4, YO, Sk2p, YO, K3, SKP (using one border and one 'body' st). 25 sts.
Row 18: Sl1 WYIF, P9, P2tog TBL, YO, P4, K1, P2tog TBL, YO, P1, P2tog TBL, YO, P2tog TBL, P1. 24 sts.
Row 19: K1, SSK, YO, SSK, K1, YO, SSK, K2tog, YO twice, SSK, K1, YO, SSK, K8, SKP (using one border and one 'body' st). 23 sts.
Row 20: Sl1 WYIF, P7, P2tog TBL, YO, P4, K1, P2tog TBL, YO, P1, P2tog TBL, YO, P2tog TBL, P1. 22 sts.
Rep Rows 1-20 for pattern.

Read the charts RS rows (numbered on the right side) from right to left, and WS rows (numbered on the left side) from left to right.

B&P (Bead and Purl)
The beads are placed using a fine steel crochet hook. To place a bead on a st, insert the hook through the hole in the bead and slide the bead up onto the hook. Pick the st off the needle with the hook and slide the bead down onto the st. Sl st back to the left needle and P.
A tutorial for this method of adding beads can be seen here: http://tutorials.knitpicks.com/knitting-with-beads-the-crochet-hook-method/.

M1P
Using the left-hand needle, pick up the bar of yarn between the needles from the back, then P the newly picked up st.

DIRECTIONS

Shawl Body
CO 3 sts.

Knit 7 rows. At the end of the last row, do not turn, but rotate the piece 90 degrees clockwise. PU and K 3 sts along the top edge; 1 st into each of the garter ridges. Rotate the piece 90 degrees clockwise again. PU and K 3 sts from the CO edge. 9 sts.

Set-up Segment with Lace Insertion
Row 1 (WS): K3, PM, (YO, K1) 3 times, YO, PM, K3. 13 sts.
Row 2 (RS): K3, SM, *K1 TBL, K1; rep from * to 1 st before M, K1 TBL, SM, K3.
Row 3: K3, SM, *P1, YO; rep from * to 1 st before M, P1, SM, K3. 19 sts.
Row 4: K3, SM, *K1, K1 TBL; rep from * to 1 st before M, K1, SM, K3.
Row 5: K3, SM, P to M, SM K3.
Row 6: K.
Row 7: Rep Row 3. 31 sts.
Row 8-10: Rep Rows 4-6.
Row 11: K3, SM, P1, *YO, P2; rep from * to M, SM, K3. 43 sts.
Row 12: K3, SM, *K2, K1 TBL; rep from * to 1 st before M, K1, SM, K3
Row 13-14: Rep Rows 5-6.
Row 15: K3, SM, P12, PM, work Geraldine Chart A beg with Row 1, PM, P12, SM, K3.
Row 16: K to second M, work Geraldine Chart A, SM, K to end.
Row 17: K3, SM, P to M, work Geraldine Chart A, SM, P to M, SM, K3.
Row 18: Rep Row 16.
Row 19: K3, SM, P1, (YO, P2) 5 times, YO, P1, SM, work Geraldine Chart A, SM, P1, (YO, P2) 5 times, YO, P1, SM, K3. 55 sts.
Row 20: K3, SM, K1, (K1 TBL, K2) 5 times, K1 TBL, K1, SM, work Geraldine Chart A, SM, K1, (K1 TBL, K2) 5 times, K1 TBL, K1, SM, K3.
Row 21: Rep Row 17.
Row 22: Rep Row 16, removing second and third M on this row.
Row 23: K3, SM, P to M, SM, K3.
Row 24: K.
Rep Rows 23-24 seven more times.

Lace Stripe 1
Set-up Row (WS): K3, SM, [K2, (YO, K1) twice] 12 times, K1, SM, K3. 79 sts.
Rows 1-3: K3, SM, work Geraldine Chart B, SM, K3.

Stockinette Stripe 1
Row 1 (WS): K3, SM, P to M, SM, K3.
Row 2 (RS): K.
Rep Rows 1-2 seven more times.

Lace Stripe 2
Set-up Row (WS): K3, SM, [K2, (YO, K1) twice] 18 times, K1, SM, K3. 115 sts.
Rows 1-7: K3, SM, work Geraldine Chart B, SM, K3.

Stockinette Stripe 2
Work as Stockinette Stripe 1.

Lace Stripe 3
Set-up Row (WS): K3, SM, [K2, (YO, K1) twice] 27 times, K1, SM, K3. 169 sts.
Rows 1-11: K3, SM, work Geraldine Chart B, SM, K3.

Stockinette Stripe 3
Work as Stockinette Stripe 1.

Lace Stripe 4
Setup Row (WS): K3, M1P, [K1, YO] twice, (K3, YO, K1, YO) 40 times, K1, M1P, SM, K3. 253 sts.
Rows 1-15: K3, SM, work Geraldine Chart B, SM, K3.

Stockinette Stripe 4
Work as Stockinette Stripe 1.

Lace Stripe 5
Set-up Row (WS): K3, M1P, [K1, YO] twice, (K3, YO, K1, YO) 61 times, K1, M1P, SM, K3. 379 sts.
Rows 1-19: K3, SM, work Geraldine Chart B, SM, K3.

Stockinette Stripe 5
Row 1 (WS): K3, SM, P to M, SM, K3.
Row 2 (RS): K.
Rep Rows 1-2 six more times.
Row 15 (WS): K3, remove M, K27, M1P, (K27, M1P, K26, M1P) 6 times, K28, remove M, K3. 392 sts. Do not cut yarn.

Border
The border is knit sideways. With each RS row worked, the last st of the border is worked together with the first st of the shawl body.

With RS facing, CO 21 sts as follows: *Insert the right needle into the first st on the left needle K-wise and pull the yarn trough. Leave the processed st on the left needle. Twist the right needle so that the processed st and the new sts are side by side, insert the left needle into the new stitch and transfer it to the left needle. Rep from * 20 more times.

Work Rows 1-20 of Geraldine Border Chart 39 times total, then rep Row 1 once more.

Turn work so that WS is facing and BO P-wise.

Finishing
Weave in ends, wash and block to diagram.

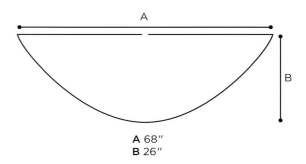

A 68"
B 26"

Border Chart

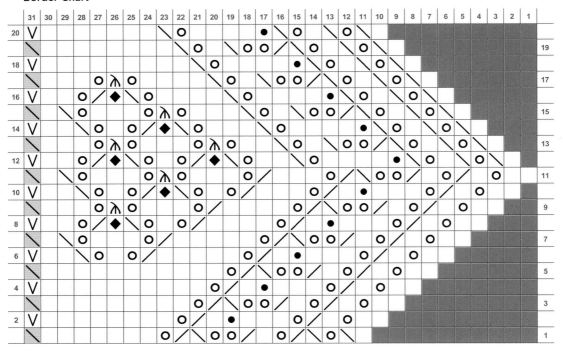

Chart A

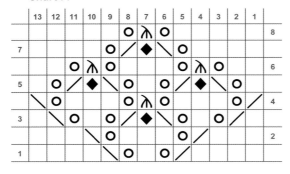

Chart B

Legend

knit
RS: knit stitch
WS: purl stitch

K2TOG
RS: Knit two stitches
together as one stitch
WS: Purl 2 stitches
together

YO
yarn over

SSK
RS: Slip one stitch as if to
knit, Slip another stitch as
if to knit. Insert left-hand
needle into front of these
2 stitches and knit them
together
WS: Purl two stitches
together TBL

pattern repeat

SKP (use last sts of
border and first st of
shawl body)

purl
RS: purl stitch
WS: knit stitch

B & P
WS: bead and purl

SK2P
slip 1, k2tog, pass slip
stitch over k2tog

S1
slip purlwise with yarn
in front

PEBBLES

by Heather Pfeifer

FINISHED MEASUREMENTS

22" wide x 59" long

YARN

Knit Picks Alpaca Cloud Lace (100% Baby Alpaca; 440 yards/50g): Anna 26760, 2 skeins

NEEDLES

US 6 (4mm) straight or 24" circular needles or longer, or size to obtain gauge

NOTIONS

Spare needle for Kitchener St
Yarn Needle
2 Stitch Markers
Scrap yarn or stitch holder

GAUGE

24 sts and 40 rows = 4" over Chart A, blocked.
18 sts and 32 rows = 4" over Charts B, C and D, blocked.
17 sts and 16 rows = 4" over Chart E, blocked

Pebbles

Notes:

This garter stitch scarf begins at the lower edging, where every WS row begins with a YO. The body is worked up from the picked-up loops along the center of the edgings. Each row of the Body begins with a YO/SSK and each half is worked to the midpoint, where both halves are grafted together. The LH and RH Edgings are picked up from loops along each edge, completing the mitered corners.

It is strongly advised to work both pieces at the same time and are referred to as Piece 1 and Piece 2.

Mark the RS of the fabric and use lifelines, according to personal preference.

The pattern is only charted. RS rows are read right to left and WS rows are read left to right.

SSK sts may be worked as K2tog TBL except when the first two stitches of a row are "YO, SSK" and except when the last stitches of Chart E join the Lace to the Body.

Garter Kitchener St

Place held sts onto spare needle. With an equal number of sts on two needles, break yarn leaving at least 3 times the width of the scarf and thread through yarn needle. Hold needles parallel, with WS's facing together and both needles pointing to the right. Front needle should have purl bumps directly beneath the needle. Back needle should have purl bumps directly beneath the needle. Both pieces have working yarn off the right edge.
Setup: Pull yarn needle P-wise through first st on front needle, leave st on knitting needle. Pull yarn needle P-wise through first st on back needle, leave st on knitting needle.
Step 1: Pull yarn needle K-wise through front st and drop st from knitting needle.
Step 2: Pull yarn needle P-wise through next front st, leave st on knitting needle.
Step 3: Pull yarn needle K-wise through first back st and drop st from knitting needle.
Step 4: Pull yarn needle P-wise through next back st, leave st on knitting needle.
Rep Steps 1-4 across all sts.
Note: Work YO sts in the same manner as other sts.

Backwards Loop CO

With needle in left hand, grasp working yarn with right hand and your thumb pointing upwards. Rotate your thumb away from you then back up to create a loop around your thumb. Slide the LH needle up under the loop and transfer st from right thumb onto LH needle. Do not pull tight.

DIRECTIONS

Knitting the two halves of the scarf simultaneously is strongly advised. When both halves are complete, graft them together using the Garter Kitchener St.

Edging (Make 2)

Note: A left leaning decrease on the RS can be worked as either SSK or K2tog TBL, however each WS Row should begin YO, SSK.

Using Backwards Loop CO, CO 5 sts.

Knit 1 row.

Work Chart A Rows 1-11 once, then Rows 12-31 five times, then Rows 32-40 once.

Using the Knitted BO method, BO all sts very loosely. 60 total loops on left edge of each Piece.

Body (make 2 - Piece 1 and Piece 2)

Instructions are the same for Piece 1 and Piece 2 except where noted.

With the YO loops from the LH of the Edging piece along the top and the sts just bound off to the right, begin working the Body.

Beginning 5 loops from the right corner, PU center 50 loops by inserting RH needle from back to front. 50 sts each Piece.

Setup Row (WS): Reattach yarn, K15, YO, K10, YO, K10, YO, K15. 3 sts inc. 53 sts each Piece.

Work Rows 1-4 of Chart B 10 times, repeating sts 6-11 seven times. 20 loops on the right and left edges of both Pieces.

Work Rows 1-30 of Chart C once.

Work Chart D Rows 1-40 of Chart D three times for Pieces 1 and 2.

Work Chart D Rows 1-19 once more on Piece 1 only.

Graft two halves together using Garter Kitchener St. 212 loops along each edge.

Lace Right Edge

Rotate piece with one set of YO loops at the top and RS facing. PU 212 loops by inserting LH needle from back to front, working from left to right along entire edge of scarf. 212 sts.

With RS facing make a slip knot and Backwards Loop CO 8 sts over right thumb onto LH needle holding the 212 sts.

Begin Chart E.
Note: The end of each RS row works one st from the Edging and one st from the Body of the scarf together. These sts must be worked as a SSK and an SK2P for Rows 9 and 31.

Work Chart E Rows 1-9 once, Rows 10-29 twenty times, and Rows 30-39 once.

BO loosely.

Lace Left Edge

Complete as for Right Edge.

Finishing

Using Mattress Stitch, seam together CO and BO edges of Lace at each corner.

Weave in ends, wash and wet block aggressively with lace wires to diagram.

Chart A

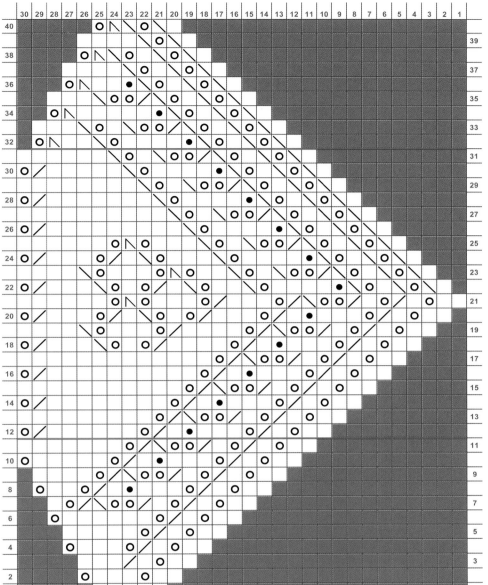

Legend

No Stitch
Placeholder - No stitch made.

knit
RS and WS: knit stitch

yo
yarn over

k2tog
RS: Knit two stitches together as one stitch
WS: Knit 2 stitches together TBL

ssk
RS: Slip one stitch as if to knit, slip another stitch as if to knit. Insert left-hand needle into front of these 2 stitches and knit them together
WS: Knit two stitches together as one stitch

purl
RS and WS: purl stitch

k3tog tbl
Knit three stitches together through back loops

sl1 k2tog psso
slip 1, k2tog, pass slip stitch over k2tog

—— **pattern repeat**

—— **stitch marker placement**

Chart B

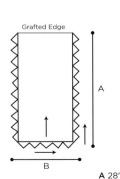
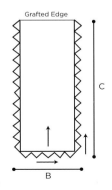

Grafted Edge

A

Grafted Edge

C

B

B

A 28″
B 22″
C 31″

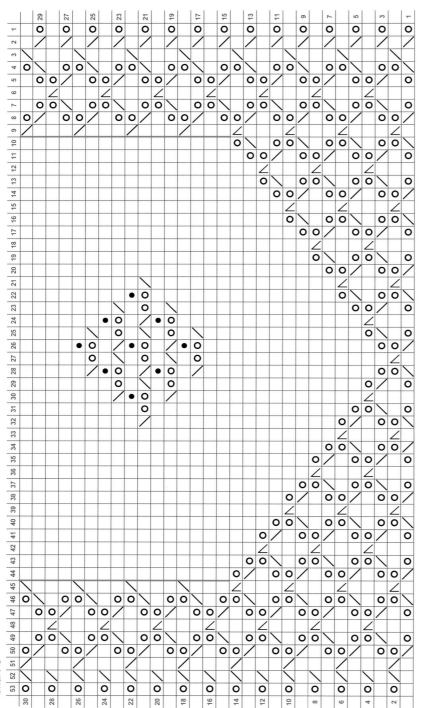

Chart C

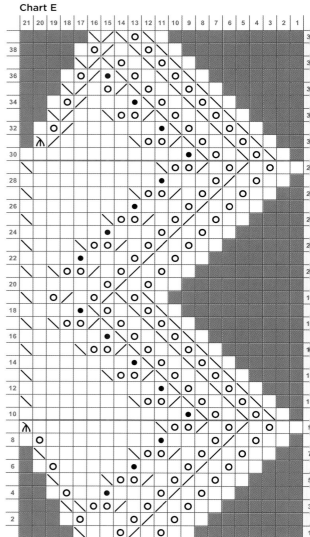

Chart E

Chart D

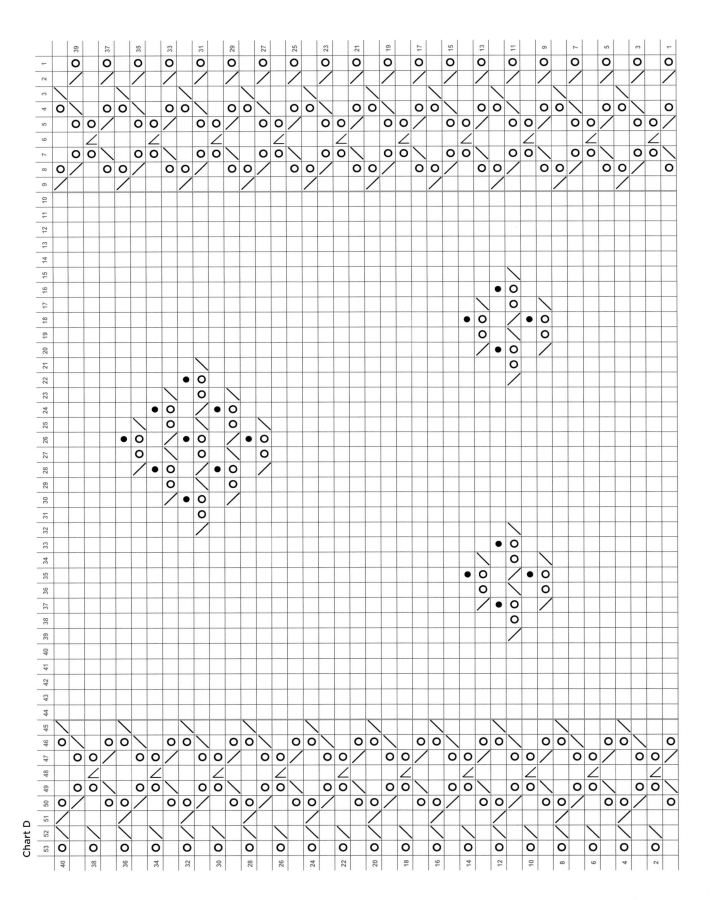

KINROSS AVENUE WRAP

by Carla Pera

FINISHED MEASUREMENTS
82" wide along lower edge x 12" high at center back

YARN
Knit Picks Luminance (100% Silk; 439 yards/50g): Brilliance 27052, 2 skeins

NEEDLES
US 3 (3.25 mm) needles, or size to obtain gauge

NOTIONS
Yarn Needle
Stitch Markers (5)
Size 6/0 seed beads, Clear with Silver Lining 81611, 1 box (optional)
US Size 11 (1.1 mm) steel crochet hook or dental floss threader for placing beads (optional)

GAUGE
28 sts and 32 rows = 4" in St st, blocked.
40 sts and 16 rows in Edging stitch pattern = 5" wide x 2.25" tall, blocked

Kinross Avenue Wrap

Notes:

The Kinross Avenue Wrap is knit as a rectangular stole with shaped ends whose gentle curve is achieved through careful blocking. The stockinette body shows off the drape and sheen of the silk yarn, while the edging features a simple lace insertion, an easy lacy faux cable stitch pattern, and an optional beaded motif, all of which are written out, as well as charted. Because it is worked side-to-side all in one piece, there is no finishing work—just bind off, weave in ends, block and look fabulous!

Make 1 Right (M1R)
Insert LH needle under strand between needles from back to front and lift strand onto needle, WYIB, insert RH needle from front to back through front of new st and knit it.

Make 1 Right Purl (M1RP)
Insert LH needle under strand between needles from back to front and lift strand onto needle, WYIF, insert RH needle from back to front through front of new st and purl it.

Place Bead and Knit (PB&K)
Use crochet hook or dental floss threader to pull stitch through the bead hole, then knit the st.

Place Bead and Purl (PB&P)
Use crochet hook or dental floss threader to pull stitch through the bead hole, then purl the st.

A tutorial for this method of adding beads can be seen here: http://tutorials.knitpicks.com/knitting-with-beads-the-crochet-hook-method/.

If beads are omitted, replace PB&K with P and PB&P with K.

If working from the chart, read the charts RS rows (odd numbers) from right to left, and WS rows (even numbers) from left to right.

Edging (worked flat over 40 sts)
Row 1 (RS): K3, SM, K9, SM, K1, K2tog, YO, K1, SM, K15, K2tog, K3, M1R, SM, K1, K2tog, YO, K1.
Row 2 (WS): K1, K2tog, YO, K1, SM, P1, M1RP, P3, P2tog, P14, SM, K1, K2tog, YO, K1, SM, P9, SM, K3.
Row 3: K3, SM, K9, SM, K1, K2tog, YO, K1, SM, K13, K2tog, K3, M1R, K2, SM, K1, K2tog, YO, K1.
Row 4: K1, K2tog, YO, K1, SM, P3, M1RP, P3, P2tog, P12, SM, K1, K2tog, YO, K1, SM, P9, SM, K3.
Row 5: K3, SM, K9, SM, K1, K2tog, YO, K1, SM, K11, K2tog, K3, M1R, K4, SM, K1, K2tog, YO, K1.
Row 6: K1, K2tog, YO, K1, SM, P5, M1RP, P3, P2tog, P10, SM, K1, K2tog, YO, K1, SM, P9, SM, K3.
Row 7: K3, SM, K4, PB&K, K4, SM, K1, K2tog, YO, K1, SM, K9, K2tog, K3, M1R, K6, SM, K1, K2tog, YO, K1.
Row 8: K1, K2tog, YO, K1, SM, P7, M1RP, P3, P2tog, P8, SM, K1, K2tog, YO, K1, SM, P3, (PB&P, P1) twice, P2, SM, K3.
Row 9: K3, SM, K2, (PB&K, K1) three times, K1, SM, K1, K2tog, YO, K1, SM, K7, K2tog, K3, M1R, K8, SM, K1, K2tog, YO, K1.
Row 10: K1, K2tog, YO, K1, SM, P9, M1RP, P3, P2tog, P6, SM, K1, K2tog, YO, K1, SM, P3, (PB&P, P1) twice, P2, SM, K3.
Row 11: K3, SM, K4, PB&K, K4, SM, K1, K2tog, YO, K1, SM, K5,

K2tog, K3, M1R, K10, SM, K1, K2tog, YO, K1.
Row 12: K1, K2tog, YO, K1, SM, P11, M1RP, P3, P2tog, P4, SM, K1, K2tog, YO, K1, SM, P9, SM, K3.
Row 13: K3, SM, K9, SM, K1, K2tog, YO, K1, SM, K3, K2tog, K3, M1R, K12, SM, K1, K2tog, YO, K1.
Row 14: K1, K2tog, YO, K1, SM, P13, M1RP, P3, P2tog, P2, SM, K1, K2tog, YO, K1, SM, P9, SM, K3.
Row 15: K3, SM, K9, SM, K1, K2tog, YO, K1, SM, K1, K2tog, K3, M1R, K14, SM, K1, K2tog, YO, K1.
Row 16: K1, K2tog, YO, K1, SM, P15, M1RP, P3, P2tog, SM, K1, K2tog, YO, K1, SM, P9, SM, K3.
Rep Rows 1-16 for pattern.

Elastic Bind-off
K first 2 sts; *Sl these sts P-wise back to left hand needle, K these 2 sts tog TBL, K next st from left hand needle; rep from * to last 2 sts; K2tog TBL; cut yarn and pull through loop.

DIRECTIONS

Left Increase Section
Using Long Tail Cast-on, CO 43 sts.
Knit 3 rows.

Setup Row (WS): K3, PM, K4, PM, K20, PM, K4, PM, K9, PM, K3.
Row 1 (RS): Work Row 1 of Edging, SM, YO, K3. 44 sts.
Row 2: K3, P to marker, SM, work Row 2 of Edging.
Row 3: Work Row 3 of Edging, SM K to last 3 sts, YO, K3. 45 sts.
Row 4: K3, P to marker, SM, work Row 4 of Edging.
Work as established until Edging Rows 1-16 have been repeated 5 times total, continuing to increase 1 st and work 3 st garter edge at end of each RS row. 91 sts.

Center Section
Row 1: Work Edging Row 1, SM, K to end.
Row 2: K3, P to M, SM, work Edging Row 2.

Work as established until Edging Rows 1-16 have been worked 24 more times.

Right Decrease Section
Row 1 (RS): Work Edging Row 1, SM, K to last 5 sts, K2tog, K3. 90 sts.
Row 2: K3, P to marker, SM, work Edging Row 2.
Work as established, decreasing 1 st and working 3 st garter edge at end of each RS row, until Edging Rows 1-16 have been worked 5 more times, then work Rows 1-14 once more.
Final Row 15: Work Edging Row 15, SM, K to last 4 sts, K2tog, K2. 43 sts.
Final Row 16: K3, SM, work Edging Row 16.
Next Row: K, remove markers as you come to them.

Knit 4 rows.

BO using Elastic Bind-off.

Finishing
Weave in ends and block gently to open out edging pattern and enhance curve.

Edging Chart

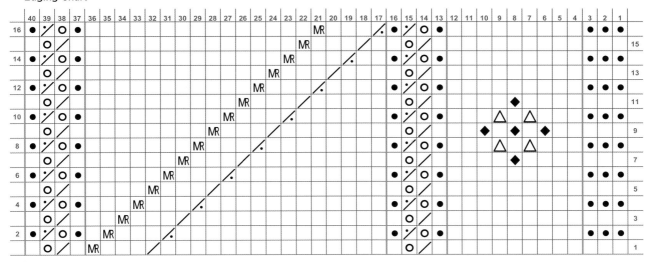

Legend

knit
RS: knit stitch
WS: purl stitch

k2tog
Knit two stitches together as one stitch

yo
yarn over

PB&P
Use crochet hook or dental floss threader to pull stitch through the bead hole, then purl the stitch

purl
RS: purl stitch
WS: knit stitch

k2tog
WS: Knit 2 stitches together as one

p2tog
RS: Purl 2 stitches together

PB&K
Use crochet hook or dental floss threader to pull stitch through the bead hole, then knit the stitch

make one right
RS: Insert LH needle under strand between needles from back to front and lift strand onto needle, WYIB, insert RH needle from front to back through front of new st and knit it

WS: Insert LH needle under strand between needles from back to front and lift strand onto needle, WYIF, insert RH needle from back to front through front of new st and purl it

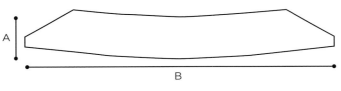

A 12″
B 82″

SYLPH

by Andrea Jurgrau

FINISHED MEASUREMENTS

Half (Three-Quarters, Full) Circle: 31.5 (31.5, 63)" back depth (diameter for Full Circle) x 63" wide at widest point

YARN

Knit Picks Luminance (100% Silk; 439 yards/50g): Reflection 27047, 3 (4, 5) skeins

NEEDLES

Half and Three-Quarters Circle Versions: US 2 (2.75mm) 40" circular needles, or size to obtain gauge
Full Circle Version: US 2 (2.75) DPNs and 16" and 40" circular needles, or size to obtain gauge

NOTIONS

Yarn Needle
Stitch Marker (Full Circle Version)
Cable needle
Waste yarn (smooth cotton) for provisional CO
0.75mm Crochet hook for adding beads
20 grams 8/0 seed beads in a color to match your yarn, Shown using Clear with Silver Lining, 81616

GAUGE

Gauge Swatch: 39 sts inc to 57 sts and 72 rows = 8.5" at CO edge increasing to 10" at Row 72" x 9" tall, over gauge swatch, blocked

Sylph

Notes:

What makes lace knitting complex? Technique? Multiple and non-repeating charts? Skinny yarn and small needles? Sylph has it all! Beads, nupps, hex mesh, and over 200 rows of non-repeating lace work. This project is a joy to knit and an heirloom once complete. It can be made as Half, Three-Quarters or Full Circle, with a delicate garter edge on all but the Full Circle, and an ornate border. The inspiration for this pattern is a short "ballet blanc" called Les Sylphides. Choreographed by Michel Fokine and with music by Frederic Chopin, the ballet is described as romantic and has no plot; sylphs dance in the moonlight with one young man.

Beads

To place beads, work stitch, slide bead onto crochet hook, lift stitch with hook, slide bead from hook to stitch, return stitch to LH needle, slip stitch to RH needle to adjust tension and work on.

Charts

Half and Three-Quarters Circle Versions: Chart RS rows (numbered on the right side) are read from right to left and WS rows (numbered on the left side) are read from left to right.
Full Circle Version: Charts A-G, all rows are read from right to left.

Double Yarn Over

Worked Flat: I did not add P stitches to the charts over the double YOs intentionally. When working flat (back and forth) you will P the first and K the second YO.
In the Round: When working in the round you will K the first and P the second YO.
If a Double YO straddles your beginning of rnd M, work a Double YO at the start of rnd, with the M between the YOs. Do not work the final YO charted in that rnd (you already worked it at the start of the round.) At the very end of the round you will K the first YO (which is actually the final stitch of the round you just completed) and make sure the M is in place to maintain your beginning of rnd. P the second YO (the first st in your new rnd). This will allow the Hex Mesh pattern to be uninterrupted at the beginning of rnd. As long as you follow these directions and keep that st marker in place it will work like magic.

Working Full Circle versus Half or Three-Quarters Versions

The Half and Three-Quarters Versions are worked flat (back and forth) while the Full Circle version is worked in the rnd.
For the Full Circle version omit the 3-st border charted on either edge of the charts and work repeats as shown in parenthesis. If no parentheses shown, work repeat as per Semi-Circle versions. The Half and Three-Quarters Versions use Charts A:1 and A:2 while the Full Circle version uses Chart A. Charts B-G are used for all versions.

Cable Twists

There are several ways to work Cable Twists without a cable needle, and that varies based on the style in which you knit.
RS Rows: you can either work them by knitting the second st, then knitting the first st, then dropping both from LH needle OR using a CN to Sl 1 st and hold it to the front of your work, K the second st, K the st from the CN.

WS Rows: you can either work them by purling the second st, then purling the first st, then drop both from LH needle OR using a CN to Sl 1 st and hold it to the front of your work, P the second st, P the st from the CN.
It doesn't matter if you do Left Cable Twists or Right Cable Twists as long as you are consistent, so feel free to use the version that is easiest for you. The pattern instructions are based on Left Cable Twists using a CN which occur in Chart A and G.

Nupps

The nupps in this project are 7-st Nupps. K the st and leave it on your LH needle. (YO, K) 3 times in the same st. Drop the st off your LH needle and continue with the row/rnd. On the return row/next rnd you will K7tog TBL when working in the round, and P7tog when working flat.

Tips for Working with Silk

Make sure your nails are smooth. Apply hand lotion before working with silk, to avoid the fibers snagging on your skin.

DIRECTIONS

Gauge Swatch

CO 39 sts using a Provisional CO.

Work Swatch Chart Rows 1-72.

Do not cut yarn. Place sts on waste yarn.

Soak swatch in cool water for 30 minutes, then roll in a towel to remove excess water. Block using 4 wires, pinning wires out to gauge dimensions.

The Gauge Swatch can be frogged to reclaim this yarn if you need it.

Half Circle Shawl (7 wedges)

With circular needle, CO 3 sts using waste yarn and a Provisional CO.

K 7 rows.

Turn work 90 degrees.

Next Row: PU and P3 along one edge, PU and K3 from Provisional CO, turn. 9 sts.
Next Row: K3, (YO, K1) 3 times, YO, K3, turn. 4 sts inc. 13 sts.
Next Row: K3, P7, K3, turn.

Work Charts A1, A2, then Chart B in sequence.

Three-Quarters Circle Shawl (9 wedges)

With circular needle, CO 3 sts using waste yarn and a Provisional CO.

K 7 rows.

Turn work 90 degrees.

Next Row: PU and P3 along one edge, PU and K3 from Provisional CO, turn. 9 sts
Next Row: K3, ((K1, YO, K1) into 1 st) 3 times, K3, turn. 6 sts inc. 15 sts.
Next Row: K3, P9, K3, turn.

Work Charts A1, A2, then Chart B in sequence.

Full Circle (12 wedges)

Using your preferred Circular CO and DPNs, CO 6 sts and join in the rnd, being careful not to twist your work.

PM for beginning of rnd. (You can initially use the yarn tail left from your CO and later place a st marker.)

Next Rnd: (M1 by K and P into the same st) 6 times. 12 sts.

Work Chart A Rnds 1-90, minding the Cable Twist details following. Switch to circular needles when convenient.

Chart A Rnds 18, 28 and 30: SM, K1, work Chart A until 2 sts before end of charted row (to the final 2-st Cable Twist), Sl 1 to CN and hold in front, remove M, K1, return st from CN to LH needle, PM.

Chart A Rnds 34 and 74: SM, K1, work Chart A until 2 sts before end of charted row (to the final 2-st Cable Twist), Sl 1 to CN and hold in front, remove M, K1, return st from CN to LH needle, YO, return M to RH needle, YO. (Pay attention to notes about Double YOs straddling beginning and end of rnds. You will have already worked the first and final YOs of Rows 35 and 75.)

Work Chart B.

For All Versions

Chart B Rows/Rnds 91-94: Work 3 st border 1 (1) (0) times. Work chart repeat 7 (9) (12) times. Work 3 st border 1 (1) (0) times.

Chart C Rows/Rnds 95-130: Work 3 st border 1 (1) (0) times. Work [section A once and 4 st section B 8 times] 7 (9) (12) times. Work section C 1 (1) (0) times. Work 3 st border 1 (1) (0) times.

Chart D Rows/Rnds 131-154: Work 3 st border 1 (1) (0) times. Work [section A once and section B 8 times] 7 (9) (12) times. Work section C 1 (1) (0) times. Work 3 st border 1 (1) (0) times.

Chart E Rows/Rnds 155-174: Work 3 st border 1 (1) (0) times. Work [section A once and section B 8 times] 7 (9) (12) times. Work section C 1 (1) (0) times. Work 3 st border 1 (1) (0) times.

Chart F Rows/Rnds 175-202: Work 3 st border 1 (1) (0) times. Work [section A once and section B 9 times] 7 (9) (12) times. Work section C 1 (1) (0) times. Work 3 st border 1 (1) (0) times.

Chart G Rows/Rnds 203-217: Work 3 st border 1 (1) (0) times. Work [section A once, section B once and section C 3 times] 6 (8) (12) times. Work [section A once and section B once] 1 (1) (0) times. Work section A 1 (1) (0) times. Work 3 st border 1 (1) (0) times.

Row 218: K (K) (P) across/around.

BO Row: K2, return 2 sts to LH needle. K2tog TBL, *return st to LH needle, K2tog TBL; rep from * until all sts are BO.

Cut yarn leaving 9″ tail and bring tail through last st, snugging it up.

Finishing

Weave in all ends on WS.

Block as follows: Soak in cool water for 30-60 minutes, until fully saturated. Press gently and roll in towel to remove excess water.

For the Half and Three-Quarters versions, use a long, flexible wire along the top edge. Pin wire.

For all versions, pin out points evenly to finished radius (31.5″).

Swatch Chart

Chart A (full circle version)

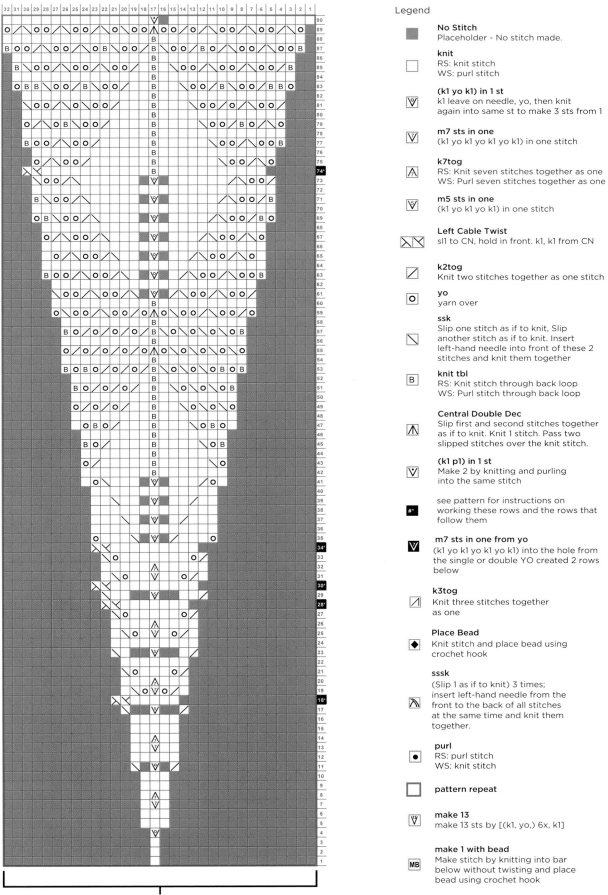

work 12 times per row

Legend

No Stitch
Placeholder - No stitch made.

knit
RS: knit stitch
WS: purl stitch

(k1 yo k1) in 1 st
k1 leave on needle, yo, then knit again into same st to make 3 sts from 1

m7 sts in one
(k1 yo k1 yo k1 yo k1) in one stitch

k7tog
RS: Knit seven stitches together as one
WS: Purl seven stitches together as one

m5 sts in one
(k1 yo k1 yo k1) in one stitch

Left Cable Twist
sl1 to CN, hold in front. k1, k1 from CN

k2tog
Knit two stitches together as one stitch

yo
yarn over

ssk
Slip one stitch as if to knit, Slip another stitch as if to knit. Insert left-hand needle into front of these 2 stitches and knit them together

knit tbl
RS: Knit stitch through back loop
WS: Purl stitch through back loop

Central Double Dec
Slip first and second stitches together as if to knit. Knit 1 stitch. Pass two slipped stitches over the knit stitch.

(k1 p1) in 1 st
Make 2 by knitting and purling into the same stitch

see pattern for instructions on working these rows and the rows that follow them

m7 sts in one from yo
(k1 yo k1 yo k1 yo k1) into the hole from the single or double YO created 2 rows below

k3tog
Knit three stitches together as one

Place Bead
Knit stitch and place bead using crochet hook

sssk
(Slip 1 as if to knit) 3 times; insert left-hand needle from the front to the back of all stitches at the same time and knit them together.

purl
RS: purl stitch
WS: knit stitch

pattern repeat

make 13
make 13 sts by [(k1, yo,) 6x, k1]

make 1 with bead
Make stitch by knitting into bar below without twisting and place bead using crochet hook

Chart A1 (half and three-quarters version)

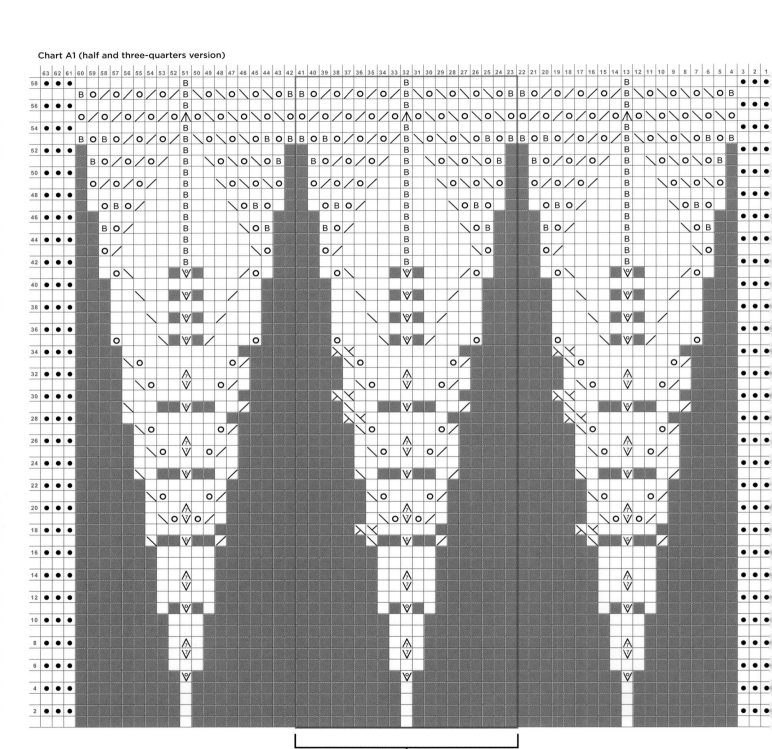

work 5 (7) times per row

Chart A2 (half and three-quarters version)

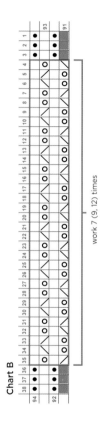

work 5 (7) times per row

Chart B

work 7 (9, 12) times

Chart C

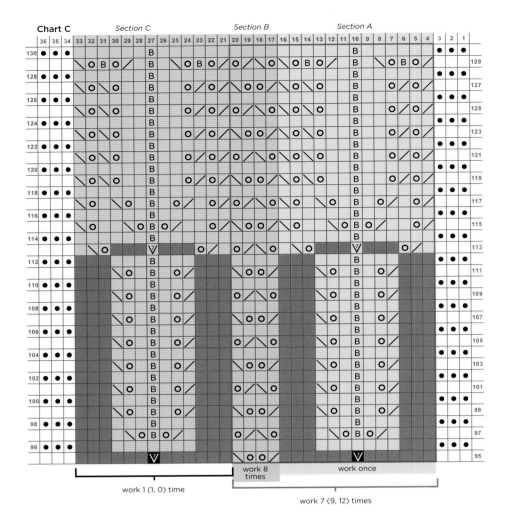

work 8 times

work once

work 1 (1, 0) time

work 7 (9, 12) times

Chart D

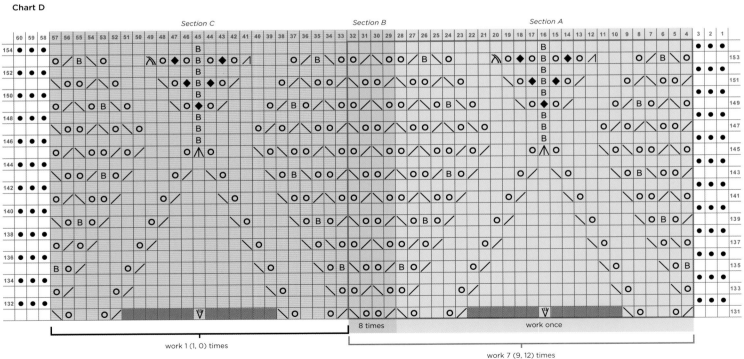

8 times

work once

work 1 (1, 0) times

work 7 (9, 12) times

Chart E

Chart F

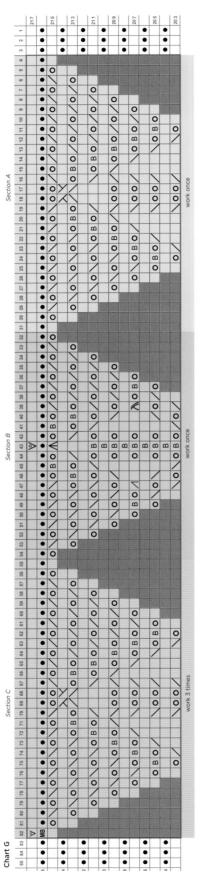

Chart G

Section A

Section B

Section C

(Work section A once, section B once and section C 3 times) 6 (8, 12) times. (Work section A once and section B once) 1 (1, 0) times. Work section A 1 (1, 0) times.

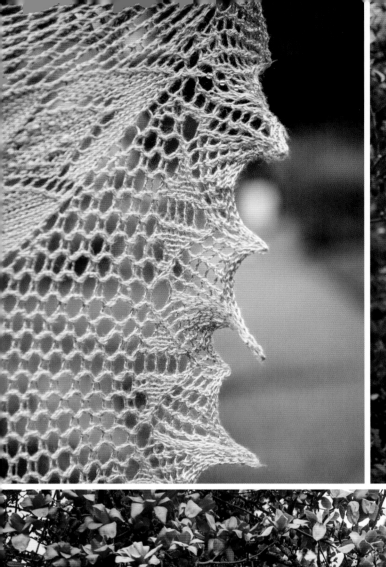

FERONIA SHAWL

by Heather Storta

FINISHED MEASUREMENTS

32 (36)" back depth, 52 (60)" wide at widest point, 82 (90)" along top neck edge

YARN

Knit Picks Gloss Lace (70% Merino Wool, 30% Silk; 440 yards/50g): Winter Night 25368, 3 (4) skeins

NEEDLES

US 5 (3.75mm) 32" circular needles or longer, or size to obtain gauge

NOTIONS

Crochet hook, size E/4
Waste yarn
Yarn needle
Stitch markers
Cable needle

GAUGE

25 sts and 32 rows = 4" over Chart A Blueberries Lace pattern, blocked.
21 sts and 28 rows = 4" over Chart B Flowers Lace pattern, blocked.
27 sts and 23 rows = 4" over Chart C Leaves Lace pattern, blocked

Feronia Shawl

Notes:

This lace shawl uses three distinct lace patterns that transition to each other. Most of the charts require lacework on both right and wrong side rows. Lace tipped needles are recommended for ease of working the decreases and cluster stitches. The design is fully customizable, as any number of repeats of Charts A, B and C may be worked before moving on to the next chart. Two sizes are listed, but feel free to adapt the pattern to any size you wish. Charts C and D create a flare to the shawl, making the overall shape a winged crescent.

P 3/3 Cluster (worked flat on the WS over 3 sts)

WYIB, Sl 3 to cable needle, wrap yarn around behind sts and to front. Repeat wrap twice more (for a total of three wraps). Yarn will be to left of sts. Slip the 3 sts back to left hand needle and P3.

Garter St (worked flat over any number of sts)

Every Row: K.

Crochet Provisional CO

Using a crochet hook and waste yarn, chain 4 sts. Using working needles and yarn, PU and K2 from the crochet chain.

Lace BO

With WS facing and working loosely, *K2togTBL. Sl the st on the right hand needle back to the left hand needle P-wise; rep from * until all sts are BO.

Working from charts

The charts do not include the Garter St edging or the center stitch. On RS rows read the chart from right to left, and on WS rows read the chart from left to right.

DIRECTIONS

Using the Crochet Provisional CO method, CO 2 sts.

K 7 rows in Garter St, ending with a WS row.

After last row, without turning work, PM, (PU and P1 along the selvege edge, PM) 3 times. PU and K2 along the CO edge, undoing the Provisional CO. 7 sts.

St markers indicate the edge sts and the center st.

All Rows: K2, SM, work appropriate lace chart beginning with Chart A to the next M, SM, work the center st TBL (K TBL on RS and P TBL on WS), SM, work appropriate lace chart beginning with Chart A to the last M, SM, K2.

Work Charts as follows:
Work Rows 1-8 of Chart A once. 23 sts.
Work Rows 9-12 of Chart A 15 times total. 263 sts.
Work Rows 1- 6 of Chart B 8 (10) times total. 391 (423) sts.
Work Rows 1-2 of Chart C once (this transitions the lace). 487 (527) sts.
Work Rows 3-8 of Chart C 6 (8) times total. 607 (687) sts.
Work Rows 1- 17 of Chart D once. 643 (723) sts.

Using Lace BO method, loosely BO all sts.

Finishing

Weave in ends, wash and block.

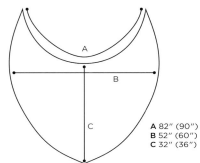

A 82" (90")
B 52" (60")
C 32" (36")

Chart A

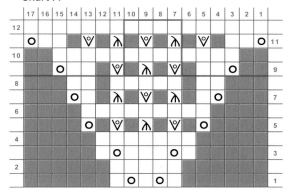

Legend

No Stitch
Placeholder - No stitch made.

yo
yarn over

knit
RS: knit stitch
WS: purl stitch

(k1 yo k1) in 1 st
k1 leave on needle, yo, then knit again into same st to make 3 sts from 1

sl1 k2tog psso
slip 1, k2tog, pass slip stitch over k2tog

pattern repeat

p3tog
Purl three stitches together as one

slip wyif
Slip stitch as if to purl, with yarn in front

p2tog tbl
Purl two stitches together in back loops, inserting needle from the left, behind and into the backs of the 2nd & 1st stitches in that order

p2tog
Purl 2 stitches together

ssk
Slip one stitch as if to knit, Slip another stitch as if to knit. Insert left-hand needle into front of these 2 stitches and knit them together

k2tog
Knit two stitches together as one stitch

(p1 yo p1) in 1 st
WS: (p1, yo, p1) all in 1 st to make 3 sts from 1

P 3/3 cluster
WS: WYIB, SI 3 to cable needle, wrap yarn around behind sts and to front. Repeat wrap twice more (for a total of three wraps). Yarn will be to left of sts. Slip the 3 sts back to left hand needle and P3.

Chart B

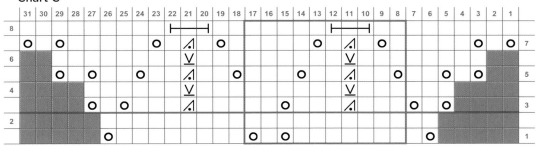

Chart C

Chart D

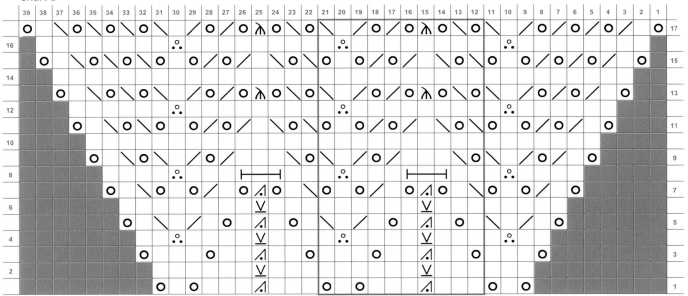

NAMIB

by Skeinwalker

FINISHED MEASUREMENTS

17.75" wide x 88" long

YARN

Knit Picks Shadow Lace (100% Merino
Wool, 440 yards/50g); Opal Heather
25366, 3 skeins

NEEDLES

US 3 (3.25mm) straight or 32" circular
needles or longer, or size to obtain gauge

NOTIONS

Yarn Needle
Size C (2.75mm) Crochet Hook
Scrap Yarn
Blocking Pins
Blocking Wires (optional)

GAUGE

20 sts and 31 rows = 4" in Sand Ripples
Pattern, blocked.
10 sts and 24 rows = 2" wide x 3" tall over
one Sand Ripples Pattern repeat, blocked.
Obtaining the gauge given is not crucial
but will affect the finished size and the
yardage needed

Namib

Notes:

This pattern is worked flat, starting from the short side and with a needle size larger than the yarn would call for. This produces a drapey, lacier fabric.

The stitch count remains constant throughout the whole pattern.

The body of the stole starts with a Provisional Crochet CO and the Sand Ripples Pattern starts right after the setup rows. The vertical borders use a minimalist yarnover st pattern that is worked at the same time as the body of the stole.

Both the lower and upper edges of the stole are worked as a knitted-on edging once the body of the stole is completed. The knitted-on edging is worked sideways starting on the RS of the work. Before starting to work the edging, place a lifeline in the body sts. This helps differentiate the body sts from the edging sts while working the edging.

For a tutorial of the Provisional Crochet CO, check the following page: http://tutorials.knitpicks.com/crocheted-provisional-cast-on/

Due to the shifting nature of the Sand Ripples Pattern, it is inconvenient to use markers as these have to be moved every other row. To catch mistakes early consider these options: (a) checking the relative position of the plain undulating lines (shown in yellow on the chart of the Sand Ripples Pattern) and the yarn overs, (b) counting the stitches per repeat on the WS rows to check that the yarn overs are at the right place.

Sand Ripples Pattern (worked flat over multiple of 10 sts plus 19)
Work Sand Ripples chart or written instructions. Sand Ripples chart shows RS rows only.
Row 1 (RS): P1, K2tog, YO, K2, SSK, K2tog, *K3, YO, K1, YO, K2, SSK, K2tog; rep from * 6 more times, K3, YO, K1, YO, K3, YO, SSK, P1. 89 sts.
Row 2 (WS): P.
Rows 3-12: Rep Rows 1-2.
Row 13 (RS): P1, K2tog, YO, K3, YO, *K1, YO, K3, SSK, K2tog, K2, YO; rep from * 6 more times, K1, YO, K3, SSK, K2tog, K2, YO, SSK, P1.
Row 14 (WS): P.
Rows 15-24: Rep Rows 13-14.
Rep Rows 1-24 for pattern.

Edging Pattern (worked flat over 6 sts)
Work Edging Chart or written instructions as follows:
Row 1 (RS): P2, YO, K2tog, K1, SSK (with one st from body). 6 sts.
Row 2 (WS): Sl1 P-wise WYIF, YO, P2tog, P3.
Rep Rows 1-2 for pattern.

Read the charts RS rows (odd numbers) from right to left, and WS rows (even numbers) from left to right.

Customizing Size
Make the stole larger or smaller by casting-on more or less sts at a multiple of 10 sts plus 19. The sample uses 7 repeats of the st pattern per row (70 sts plus 19). Adjust this number to the desired target width. For a scarf width of 7.25", use 2 repeats (20 sts plus 19) instead of 7.

Make the stole taller or shorter by working more or less row repeats. Add or remove repeats of Sand Ripples Pattern, then proceed to work as instructed for the Edging.
As the yardage needed varies heavily from knitter to knitter, you can use a scale to determine the extra yardage needed per repeat.

DIRECTIONS

Setup
With crochet hook, one knitting needle, scrap yarn, and Provisional Crochet CO method, CO 89 sts.

K 2 rows, ending with a WS row.

Body
Work Sand Ripples Pattern Rows 1-24 twenty-eight times.

Transition rows
P 2 rows, ending with a WS row, don't turn work.

Edging
With working yarn and WS facing, CO 6 sts loosely with a Backward Loop CO, spacing the stitches equally, turn work.

Setup Row 1 (RS): P2, K3, K2tog (with one st from body).
Setup Row 2 (WS): Sl1 P-wise WYIF, P5.

Work Edging Pattern until 2 sts from the body remain. 172 edging rows.

Finishing Row 1 (RS): P2, K3, K2tog, Sl1 P-wise WYIB.
Finishing Row 2 (WS): BO loosely as follows: Sl1 P-wise WYIB, P1, PSSO, *P1, PPSO; rep from * until all sts are BO. Cut yarn and pull end through last st.

Work the edging along the CO edge as follows. Hold the stole by the corners of the CO edge with WS facing. Then with WS still facing, pick up the live sts from right to left, carefully unravelling the Provisional CO (the tail is on the right side of the work). At the very end, pick up one more loop. Don't turn the work. 89 sts.

With WS still facing, CO 6 sts loosely with a backward-loop CO spacing the stitches equally. Turn the work.

Work the Edging Setup Rows 1 & 2, the Edging Pattern and the Edging Finishing Rows 1 & 2 as previously.

Finishing
Weave in and secure all ends. Wash and block to final measurements plus 0.25" as the work will spring back when released from the blocking pins.

Align all the crests on each side of the stole and stretch them all to the same distance. Block with four pins per crest along the long edge to get nicely rounded edges. Or if using blocking wires, thread the wires in the yarn overs of all edges. Then use two pins per crest to unfold the border stitches.

Sand Ripples Chart

29	28	27	26	25	24	23	22	21	20	19	18	17	16	15	14	13	12	11	10	9	8	7	6	5	4	3	2	1	
●	\	O			/	\				O		O			/	\				O		O				O	/	●	23
●	\	O			/	\				O		O			/	\				O		O				O	/	●	21
●	\	O			/	\				O		O			/	\				O		O				O	/	●	19
●	\	O			/	\				O		O			/	\				O		O				O	/	●	17
●	\	O			/	\				O		O			/	\				O		O				O	/	●	15
●	\	O			/	\				O		O			/	\				O		O				O	/	●	13
●	\	O				O		O				/	\			O		O				/	\			O	/	●	11
●	\	O				O		O				/	\			O		O				/	\			O	/	●	9
●	\	O				O		O				/	\			O		O				/	\			O	/	●	7
●	\	O				O		O				/	\			O		O				/	\			O	/	●	5
●	\	O				O		O				/	\			O		O				/	\			O	/	●	3
●	\	O				O		O				/	\			O		O				/	\			O	/	●	1

Legend

- **purl** — purl stitch (●)
- **knit** — knit stitch (□)
- **edge stitches**
- **k2tog** — RS: Knit two stitches together as one stitch; WS: Purl two stitches together as one stitch (/)
- **ssk** — Slip one stitch as if to knit, slip another stitch as if to knit. Insert left-hand needle into front of these 2 stitches and knit them together (\)
- **pattern repeat**
- **yo** — yarn over (O)
- **vertical undulating line**
- **slip wyif** — Slip stitch as if to purl, with yarn in front (V)
- **ssk with 1 st of stole body**

Edging Chart

6	5	4	3	2	1	
V	O	/				2
(ssk w/ body)		/	O	●	●	1

Direction of knitting (body) →

Direction of knitting (edging) ↓

w

l

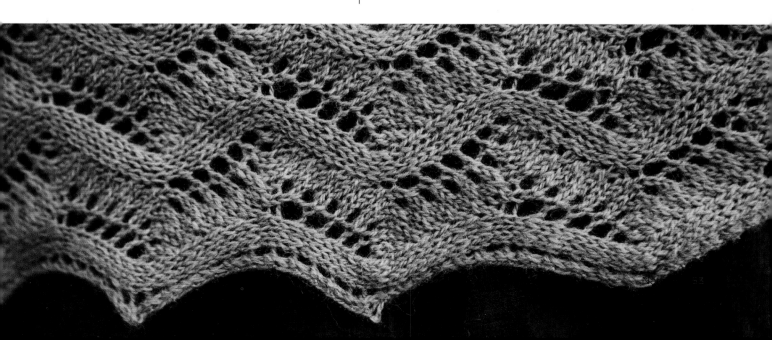

DIAMONDS OF EOS

by Kristi Holaas

FINISHED MEASUREMENTS

41" back depth, x 88" wide at widest point

YARN

Knit Picks Shimmer Bare (70% Baby Alpaca, 30% Silk; 880 yards/100g): Bare Shimmer 26584, 2 skeins

NEEDLES

US 4 (3.5mm) 32" or longer circular needles, or size to obtain gauge
US 7 (4.5mm) 32" or longer circular needles, or 3 sizes larger than size to obtain gauge

NOTIONS

Yarn Needle
Stitch Markers in 2 colors: A and B

GAUGE

18 sts and 21 rows = 4" over Diamonds of Eos Chart Two pattern with smaller needles, blocked

Diamonds of Eos

Notes:

Diamonds of Eos is a triangular shawl worked flat from the bottom edge upwards. Shaping is accomplished by decreasing at each edge of the two sections on either side of the center spine lace pattern. Traditional Estonian stitches and stitch patterns are used to create striking and very distinct sections in this large heirloom shawl.

Charts are read from right to left on odd number RS rows and left to right on even number WS rows.

Color A and/or B markers (also called out as "A Markers" and "B Markers" are placed as written for each chart. Slipping the markers are not included in the directions unless they are an integral part of the instruction.

Nupp

Very sharp tipped needles are recommended to help in creating the traditional 5 stitch Nupp.

Nupp St: On RS, K1, YO, K1, YO, K1 in 1 st, when you come to these sts on the WS row slide the 5 sts to the end of the needle tip very carefully. P5tog to form the completed Nupp resulting in 1 st.

Set up Chart:

Row 1 (RS): Sl1, KFB, YO, K8, SKP, K9, (YO, K9, SKP, K9) 29 times, YO, K9, Sk2p, K8, YO, KFB Sl1. 2 sts inc. 625 sts.

Row 2 (WS): P1, K2, P to last 3 sts, K2, P1.

Row 3: Sl1, KFB, K1, YO, SKP, K6, Sk2p, K6, K2tog, YO, (K1, YO, SKP, K6, Sk2p, K6, K2tog, YO) 29 times, K1, YO, SKP, K6, Sk2p, K6, K2tog, YO, K1, KFB, Sl1.

Row 4: P1, K3, P to last 4 sts, K3, P1. 60 sts dec. 565 sts.

Row 5: Sl1, KFB, K3, YO, SKP, K4, Sk2p, K4, K2tog, YO, K1, (K2, YO, SKP, K4, Sk2p, K4, K2tog, YO, K1) 29 times, K2, YO, SKP, K4, Sk2p, K4, K2tog, YO, K3, KFB, Sl1. 60 sts dec. 505 sts.

Row 6: P1, K4, P to last 5 sts, K4, P1.

Chart One:

Row 1(RS): Sl1, K4, YO, SKP, K4, Sk2p, K4, YO, K2tog, YO, (K1, YO, SKP, YO, K4, Sk2p, K4, YO, K2tog, YO) 14 times, K1, YO, SKP, YO, K4, Sk2p, K4, YO, K2tog, YO, (K1, YO, SKP, YO, K4, Sk2p, K4, YO, K2tog, YO) 14 times, K1, YO, SKP, YO, K4, Sk2p, K4, YO, K2tog, YO, K4, Sl1.

Rows 2-8 Even Rows (WS): P1, K4, P to last 5 sts, K4, P1.

Row 3: SL1, K5, YO, SKP, YO, K3, Sk2p, K3, YO, K2tog, YO, K1, (K2, YO, SKP, YO, K3, Sk2p, K3, YO, K2tog, YO, K1) 14 times, K2, YO, SKP, YO, K3, Sk2p, K3, YO, K2tog, YO, K1, (K2, YO, SKP, YO, K3, Sk2p, K3, YO, K2tog, YO, K1) 14 times, K2, YO, SKP, YO, K3, Sk2p, K3, YO, K2tog, YO, K5, Sl1.

Row 5: Sl1, K6, YO, SKP, YO, K2, Sk2p, K2, YO, K2tog, YO, K2, (K3, YO, SKP, YO, K2, Sk2p, K2, YO, K2tog, YO, K2) 14 times, K3, YO, Sk2p, YO, K1, Sk2p, K1, YO, K3tog, YO, K2, (K3, YO, SKP, YO, K2, Sk2p, K2, YO, K2tog, YO, K2) 14 times, K3, YO, SKP, YO, K2, Sk2p, K2, YO, K2tog, YO, K6, Sl1.

Row 7: Sl1, K7, YO, SKP, YO, K1, Sk2p, K1, YO, K2tog, YO, K3, (K4, YO, SKP, YO, K1, Sk2p, K1, YO, K2tog, YO, K3) 14 times, K4, SKP, YO, Sk2p, YO, K2tog, K3, (K4, YO, SKP, YO, K1, Sk2p, K1, YO, K2tog, YO, K3) 14 times, K4, YO, SKP, YO, K1, Sk2p, K1, YO, K2tog,

YO, K7, Sl1.

Row 9: Sl1, K8, YO, SKP, YO, Sk2p, YO, K2tog, YO, (K1, YO, K2, Sk2p, K2, YO, K1, YO, SKP, YO, Sk2p, YO, K2tog, YO) 14 times, remove last A Marker and replace with a B Marker, K7, K2tog, K3, SKP, K7, remove A Marker, replace with a B Marker, (YO, SKP, YO, Sk2p, YO, K2tog, YO, K1, YO, K2, Sk2p, K2, YO, K1)14 times, YO, SKP, YO, Sk2p, YO, K2tog, YO, K8, Sl1.

Row 10: P1, K4, P to 7 sts past first B Marker, K1, P3, K1, P to last 5 sts, K4, P1.

Row 11: Sl1, K9, YO, SKP, K1, K2tog, YO, K1, (Nupp, K1, YO, K1, Sk2p, K1, YO, K1, Nupp, K1, YO, SKP, K1, K2tog, YO, K1) 14 times, K5, K3tog, YO, Sk2p, YO, Sk2p, K5, (K1, YO, SKP, K1, K2tog, YO, K1, Nupp, K1, YO, K1, Sk2p, K1, YO, K1, Nupp) 14 times, K1, YO, SKP, K1, K2tog, YO, K9, Sl1.

Row 12: P1, K4, P to 5 sts past first B Marker, K1, P3, K1, P to last 5 sts, K4, P1.

Row 13: Sl1, K3, SKP, K5, YO, Sk2p, YO, (K1, YO, SKP, Nupp, K1, YO, Sk2p, YO, K1, Nupp, K2tog, YO, K1, YO, Sk2p, YO) 14 times, K5, K3tog, YO, K3, YO, Sk2p, K5, (YO, Sk2p, YO, K1, YO, SKP, Nupp, K1, YO, Sk2p, YO, K1, Nupp, K2tog, YO, K1) 14 times, YO, Sk2p, YO, K5, K2tog, K3, Sl1.

Row 14: P1, K4, P to 5 sts past first B Marker, K1, P5, K1, P to last 5 sts, K4, P1.

Row 15: Sl1, K3, SKP, K5, Nupp, K1, (K2, YO, SKP, Nupp, K3, Nupp, K2tog, YO, K3, Nupp, K1) 14 times, K3, K3tog, YO, K5, YO, Sk2p, K3, (K1, Nupp, K3, YO, SKP, Nupp, K3, Nupp, K2tog, YO, K2) 14 times, K1, Nupp, K5, K2tog, K3, Sl1.

Row 16: P1, K4, P to 3 sts past first B Marker, K1, P7, K1, P to last 5 sts K4, P1.

Row 17: Sl1, K3, SKP, K3, Nupp, K1, Nupp, (K3, YO, SKP, Nupp, K1, Nupp, K2tog, YO, K3, Nupp, K1, Nupp) 14 times, K1, K3tog, YO, K3, Nupp, K3, YO, Sk2p, K1, (Nupp, K1, Nupp, K3, YO, SKP, Nupp, K1, Nupp, K2tog, YO, K3) 14 times, Nupp, K1, Nupp, K3, K2tog, K3, Sl1.

Row 18: P1, K4, P to 1 st past first B Marker, K1, P9, K1, P to last 5 sts, K4, P1.

Row 19: Sl1, K3, SKP, K3, Nupp, (K5, YO, SKP, Nupp, K2tog, YO, K5, Nupp) 14 times, K1, K2tog, YO, K3, Nupp, K1, Nupp, K3, YO, SKP, K1, (Nupp, K5, YO, SKP, Nupp, K2tog, YO, K5) 14 times, Nupp, K3, K2tog, K3, Sl1.

Row 20: P1, K4, P to 1 st past first B Marker, K1, P11, K1, P to last 5 sts, K4, P1.

Row 21: Sl1, K3, SKP, K3, (K6, YO, Sk2p, YO, K7) 14 times, K3, YO, SKP, K2, Nupp, K2, K2tog, YO, K3, (K7, YO, Sk2p, YO, K6) 14 times, K3, K2tog, K3, Sl1. 479 sts

Row 22: P1, K4, P to first B Marker, K1, P13, K1, P to last 5 sts, K4, P1.

Chart Two:

Row 1 (RS): Sl1, K3, SKP, remove A Markers as you K225, remove B Marker, K2tog, place B Marker, K3, YO, SKP, K3, K2tog, YO, K3, remove next B Marker and place here, SKP, K225, K2tog, K3, Sl1.

Rows 2&4 (WS): P1, K to first B Marker, P13, K to last st, P1.

Row 3: Sl1, K3, SKP, K to 2 sts before first B Marker, K2tog, K4, YO, SKP, K1, K2tog, YO, K4, SKP, K to last 6 sts, K2tog, K3, Sl1.

Row 5: Sl1, K3, SKP, K to 2 sts before first B Marker, K2tog, K5, YO, Sk2p, YO, K5, SKP, K to last 6 sts, K2tog, K3, Sl1.

Row 6: P1, K4, P to 1 st before B Marker, K1, P13, K1, P to last 5 sts,

K4, P1.

Tip: Keep your tension a little loose on Row 6. It will make the 3-into-3 sts much easier to complete.

Row 7: Sl1, K3, SKP, 3-into-3 73 times (this should end up 2 sts before B Marker), K2tog, K4, Nupp, K3, Nupp, K4, SKP, 3-into-3 73 times, K2tog, K3, Sl1.

Row 8-16 Even Rows (WS): P1, K4, P to 1 st before B Marker, K1, P13, K1, P to last 5 sts, K4, P1.

Row 9: Sl1, K3, SKP, K to 2 sts before first B Marker, K2tog, K3, Nupp, K5, Nupp, K3, SKP, K to last 6 sts, K2tog, K3, Sl1.

Row 11: Sl1, K3, SKP, P to 2 sts before first B Marker, K2tog, K2, Nupp, K2, K2tog, YO, K3, Nupp, K2, SKP, P to last 6 sts, K2tog, K3, Sl1.

Row 13: Sl1, K3, SKP, P to 2 sts before B Marker, K2tog, K1, Nupp, K2, K2tog, YO, K2tog, YO, K3, Nupp, K1, SKP, P to last 6 sts, K2tog, K3, Sl1. 447 sts.

Row 15: Sl1, K3, SKP, K to 2 sts before B Marker K2tog, K2, Nupp, K2, K2tog, YO, K3, Nupp, K2, SKP, K to last 6 sts, K2tog, K3, Sl1.

Chart Three:

Row 1 (RS): Sl1, K3, SKP, K2, (Nupp, K11) 17 times, Nupp, K2, K2tog, K3, Nupp, K5, Nupp, K3, SKP, K2, (Nupp, K11) 17 times, Nupp, K2, K2tog, K3, Sl1. 447 sts.

Row 2-28, Even rows (WS): P1, K4, P to 1 st before first B Marker, K1, P13, K1, P to last 5 sts, K4, P1.

Row 3: Sl1, K3, SKP, K1, (K2, YO, SKP, K1, 3-into-3, K1, K2tog, YO, K1) 17 times, K2, K2tog, K4, Nupp, K3, Nupp, K4, SKP, K1, (K2, YO, SKP, K1, 3-into-3, K1, K2tog, YO, K1) 17 times, K2, K2tog, K3, Sl1.

Row 5: Sl1, K3, SKP, (K1, YO, SKP, YO, SKP, K3, K2tog, YO, K2tog, YO) 17 times, K1, K2tog, K5, YO, Sk2p, YO, K5, SKP, (K1, YO, SKP, YO, SKP, K3, K2tog, YO, K2tog, YO) 17 times, K1, K2tog, K3, Sl1.

Row 7: Sl1, K3, SKP, K1, YO, SKP, YO, SKP, K1, K2tog, YO, K2tog, YO, K1, (K2, YO, SKP, YO, SKP, K1, K2tog, YO, K2tog, YO, K1) 16 times, K2tog, K3, K2tog, YO, K3, YO, SKP, K3, SKP, K1, YO, SKP, YO, SKP, K1, K2tog, YO, K2tog, YO, K1, (K2, YO, SKP, YO, SKP, K1, K2tog, YO, K2tog, YO, K1) 16 times, K2tog, K3, Sl1.

Row 9: Sl1, K3, SKP, K1, YO, SKP, YO, Sk2p, YO, K2tog, YO, K2, (K3, YO, SKP, YO, Sk2p, YO, K2tog, YO, K2) 15 times, K3, YO, SKP, YO, Sk2p, YO, K2tog, YO, K1, K2tog, K2, K2tog, YO, K5, YO, SKP, K2, SKP, K1, Yo, SKP, YO, Sk2p, YO, K2tog, YO, K2, (K3, YO, SKP, YO, Sk2p, YO, K2tog, K2) 15 times, K3, YO, YO, SKP, YO, Sk2p, YO, K2tog, YO, K1, K2tog, K3, Sl1.

Row 11: Sl1, K3, SKP, K1, YO, SKP, (place A Marker, K1, K2tog, YO, K3, remove A Marker, Nupp, K3, YO, SKP, K1, K2tog, YO, K2, K2tog, YO, K3, YO, SKP) 8 times, K1, K2tog, YO, K1, K2tog, K1, K2tog, YO, K3, Nupp, K3, YO, SKP, K1, SKP, K1, YO, SKP, (place A Marker, K1, K2tog, YO, K2, K2tog, remove A Marker, YO, K3, YO, SKP, K1, K2tog, YO, K3, remove A Marker, Nupp, K3, YO, SKP) 8 times, K1, K2tog YO, K1, K2tog, K3, Sl1.

Row 13: Sl1, K3, SKP, K2, (Nupp, K4, Nupp, K1, Nupp, K4, Nupp, K3, K2tog, YO, K2tog, YO, K4, Nupp, K4) 8 times, Nupp, K2, K2tog, K2tog, YO, K3, Nupp, K1, Nupp, K3, YO, SKP, SKP, K2, (Nupp, K3, K2tog, YO, K2tog, YO, K4, Nupp, K4, Nupp, K1, Nupp, K4) 8 times, Nupp, K2, K2tog, K3, Sl1.

Row 15: Sl1, K3, SKP, K1, (K6, Nupp, K10, K2tog, YO, K5) 8 times, K2, K2tog, K2, YO, SKP, K2, Nupp, K2, K2tog, YO, K2, SKP, K1, (K5, K2tog, YO, K11, Nupp, K5) 8 times, K2, K2tog, K3, Sl1.

Row 17: Sl1, K3, SKP, remove A Marker, K2, YO, SKP, K2, (place A Marker, K3, K2tog, YO, K3, YO, SKP, K2) 15 times removing extra A Markers as needed, K3, K2tog, YO, K2, K2tog, K3, YO, SKP, K3, K2tog, YO, K3, SKP, remove A Marker, K2, YO, SKP, K2, (place A Marker, K3, K2tog, YO, K3, YO, SKP, K2) 15 times removing extra A Markers as needed, K3, K2tog, YO, K2, K2tog, K3, Sl1.

Row 19: Sl1, K3, SKP, YO, SKP, YO, SKP, K1, (K2, K2tog, YO, K2tog, YO, K1, YO, SKP, YO, SKP, K1) 15 times, K2, K2tog, YO, K2tog, YO, K2tog, K4, YO, SKP, K1, K2tog, YO, K4, SKP, YO, SKP, YO, SKP, K1, (K2, K2tog, YO, K2tog, YO, K1, YO, SKP, YO, SKP, K1) 15 times, K2, K2tog, YO, K2tog, YO, K2tog, K3, Sl1.

Row 21: Sl1, K3, SKP, YO, SKP, YO, SKP, (K1, K2tog, YO, K2tog, YO, K3, YO, SKP, YO, SKP) 15 times, K1, K2tog, YO, K2tog, YO, K2tog, K5, YO, Sk2p, YO, K5, SKP, YO, SKP, YO, SKP, (K1, K2tog, YO, K2tog, YO, K3, YO, SKP, YO, SKP) 15 times, K1, K2tog, YO, K2tog, YO, K2tog, K3, Sl1.

Row 23: Sl1, K3, SKP, YO, SKP, YO, Sl A Marker as needed (Sk2p, YO, K2tog, YO, K1, 3-into-3, K1, YO, SKP, YO, Sl A Marker as needed) 15 times, Sk2p, YO, K2tog, YO, K2tog, K4, Nupp, K3, Nupp, K4, SKP, YO, SKP, YO, Sl A Marker as needed (Sk2p, YO, K2tog, YO, K1, 3-into-3, K1, YO, SKP, YO, Sl A Marker as needed) 15 times, Sk2p, YO, K2tog, YO, K2tog, K3, Sl1.

Row 25: Sl1, K3, SKP, YO, SKP, (K1, K2tog, YO, K7, YO, SKP) 15 times, K1, K2tog, YO, K2tog, K3, Nupp, K5, Nupp, K3, SKP, YO, SKP, (K1, K2tog, YO, K7, YO, SKP) 15 times, K1, K2tog, YO, K2tog, K3, Sl1.

Row 27: Sl1, K3, SKP, K1, (Nupp, K11) 15 times, Nupp, K1, K2tog, K2, Nupp, K2, K2tog, YO, K3, Nupp, K2, SKP, K1, (Nupp, K11) 15 times, Nupp, K1, K2tog, K3, Sl1. 391 sts.

Chart Four:

Row 1 (RS): Sl1, K3, SKP, K to 2 sts before first B Marker, K2tog, K1, Nupp, K2, K2tog, YO, K2tog, YO, K3, Nupp, K1, SKP, K to last 6 sts, K2tog, K3, Sl1. 387 sts.

Rows 2&4 (WS): P1, K to 1 st before first B Marker, K1, P13, K to last st, P1.

Row 3: Sl1, K3, SKP, K to 2 sts before first B Marker, K2tog, K2, Nupp, K2, K2tog, YO, K3, Nupp, K2, SKP, K to last 6 sts, K2tog, K3, Sl1.

Row 5: Sl1, K3, SKP, K to 2 sts before first B Marker, K2tog, K3, Nupp, K5, Nupp, K3, SKP, K to last 6 sts, K2tog, K3, Sl1.

Rows 6-16 Even rows (WS): P1, K4, P to 1 st before first B Marker, K1, P13, K1, P to last 5 sts, K4, P1.

Row 7: Sl1, K3, SKP, K1, 3-into-3 58 times, K2tog, K4, Nupp, K3, Nupp, K4, SKP, 3-into-3 58 times, K1, K2tog, K3, Sl1.

Row 9: Sl1, K3, SKP, K to 2 sts before first B Marker, K2tog, K5, YO, Sk2p, YO, K5, SKP, K to last 6 sts, K2tog, K3, Sl1.

Row 11: Sl1, K3, SKP, P to 2 sts before first B Marker, K2tog, K3, K2tog, YO, K3, YO, SKP, K3, SKP, P to last 6 sts, K2tog, K3, Sl1.

Row 13: Sl1, K3, SKP, P to 2 sts before first B Marker, K2tog, K2, K2tog, YO, K5, YO, SKP, K2, SKP, P to last 6 sts, K2tog, K3, Sl1.

Row 15: Sl1, K3, SKP, K to 2 sts before first B Marker, K2tog, K1, K2tog, YO, K3, Nupp, K3, YO, SKP, K1, SKP, K to last 6 sts, K2tog, K3, Sl1. 359 sts.

Chart Five - Sides Chart:

Row 1 (RS): Sl1, K3, SKP, K5, K2tog, YO, K1, YO, SKP, K2, (K3, K2tog, YO, K1, YO, SKP, K2), K3, K2tog, YO, K1, YO, SKP, K5, (CS),

K5, K2tog, YO, K1, YO, SKP, K2, (K3, K2tog, YO, K1, YO, SKP, K2), K3, K2tog, YO, K1, YO, SKP, K5, K2tog, K3, SI1.

Rows 2-12 Even rows (WS): P1, K4, P to 1 st before first B Marker, K1, P13, K1, P to last 5 sts, K4, P1.

Row 3: SI1, K3, K2tog, YO, K1, Nupp, K1, YO, SKP, K1, (K2, K2tog, YO, K1, Nupp, K1, YO, SKP, K1), K2, K2tog, YO, K1, Nupp, K1, YO, SKP, K3, (CS), K3, K2tog, YO, K1, Nupp, K1, YO, SKP, K1, (K2, K2tog, YO, K1, Nupp, K1, YO, SKP, K1), K2, K2tog, YO, K1, Nupp, K1, YO, SKP, K3, K2tog, K3, SI1.

Row 5: SI1, K3, SKP, K1, K2tog, YO, K1, Nupp, K1, Nupp, K1, YO, SKP, (K1, K2tog, YO, K1, Nupp, K1, Nupp, K1, YO, SKP), K1, K2tog, YO, K1, Nupp, K1, Nupp, K1, YO, SKP, K1, (CS), K1, K2tog, YO, K1, Nupp, K1, Nupp, K1, YO, SKP, (K1, K2tog, YO, K1, Nupp, K1, Nupp, K1, YO, SKP), K1, K2tog, YO, K1, Nupp, K1, Nupp, K1, YO, SKP, K1, K2tog, K3, SI1.

Row 7: SI1, K3, SKP, K1, YO, SKP, K1, Nupp, K1, K2tog, YO, K1, (K2, YO, SKP, K1, Nupp, K1, K2tog, YO, K1), K2, YO, SKP, K1, Nupp, K1, K2tog, YO, K1, (CS), K1, YO, SKP, K1, Nupp, K1, K2tog, YO, K1, (K2, YO, SKP, K1, Nupp, K1, K2tog, YO, K1), K2, YO, SKP, K1,, Nupp, K1, K2tog, YO, K1, K2tog, K3, SI1.

Row 9: SI1, K3, SKP, K1, YO, SKP, K1, K2tog, YO, K2, (K3, YO, SKP, K1, K2tog, YO, K2), K3, YO, SKP, K1, K2tog, YO, (CS), K1, YO, SKP, K1, K2tog, YO, K2, (K3, YO, SKP, K1, K2tog, YO, K2), K3, YO, SKP, K1, K2tog, YO, K1, K2tog, K3, SI1.

Row 11: SI1, K3, SKP, K1, YO, Sk2p, YO, K1, K2tog, YO, (K1, YO, SKP, K1, YO, Sk2p, YO, K1, K2tog, YO), K1, YO, SKP, K1, YO, Sk2p, YO, K1, (CS), K1, YO, Sk2p, YO, K1, K2tog, YO, (K1, YO, SKP, K1, YO, Sk2p, YO, K1, K2tog, YO), K1, YO, SKP, K1, YO, Sk2p, YO, K1, K2tog, K3, SI1.

Repeat Rows 3-12 for pattern.

Chart Five - Center Spine (CS) Chart:

Row 1 (RS): K2tog, K2tog, YO, K3, Nupp, K1, Nupp, K3, YO, SKP, SKP.

Rows 2-32 Even Rows (WS): K1, P13, K1.

Row 3: K2tog, K2, YO, SKP, K2, Nupp, K2, K2tog, YO, K2, SKP.

Row 5: K2tog, K3, YO, SKP, K3, K2tog, YO, K3, SKP.

Row 7: K2tog, K4, YO, SKP, K1, K2tog, YO, K4, SKP.

Row 9: K2tog, K5, YO, Sk2p, YO, K5, SKP.

Row 11: K2tog, K4, Nupp, K3, Nupp, K4, SKP.

Row 13: K2tog, K3, Nupp, K5, Nupp, K3, SKP.

Row 15: K2tog, K2, Nupp, K2, K2tog, YO, K3, Nupp, K2, SKP.

Row 17: K2tog, K1, Nupp, K2, K2tog, YO, K2tog, YO, K3, Nupp, K1, SKP.

Row 19: K2tog, K2, Nupp, K2, K2tog, YO, K3, Nupp, K2, SKP.

Row 21: K2tog, K3, Nupp, K5, Nupp, K3, SKP.

Row 23: K2tog, K4, Nupp, K3, Nupp, K4, SKP.

Row 25: K2tog, K5, YO, Sk2p, YO, K5, SKP.

Row 27: K2tog, K3, K2tog, YO, K3, YO, SKP, K3, SKP.

Row 29: K2tog, K2, K2tog, YO, K5, YO, SKP, K2, SKP.

Row 31: K2tog, K1, K2tog, YO, K3, Nupp, K3, YO, SKP, K1, SKP.

Repeat Rows 1-32 for pattern.

Chart Six:

Row 1 (RS): SI1, K3, SKP, (K3, K2tog, YO, K1, Nupp, K1, YO, SKP) 2 times, K3, K2tog, K2, Nupp, K2, K2tog, YO, K3, Nupp, K2, SKP, (K3, K2tog, YO, K1, Nupp, K1, YO, SKP) times 2, K3, K2tog, K3, SI1. 75sts.

Rows 2&4 (WS): P1, K4, P to 1 st before first B Marker, K1, P13, K1, P to last 5 sts, K4, P1.

Row 3: SI1, K3, SKP, (K1, K2tog, YO, K1, Nupp, K1, Nupp, K1, YO, SKP) 2 times, K1, K2tog, K1, Nupp, K2, K2tog, YO, K2tog, YO, K3, Nupp, K1, SKP, (K1, K2tog, YO, K1, Nupp, K1, Nupp, K1, YO, SKP) 2 times, K1, K2tog, K3, SI1.

Row 5: SI1, K3, SKP, K1, YO, SKP, K1, Nupp, K1, K2tog, YO, K3, YO, SKP, K1, Nupp, K1, K2tog, YO, K1, K2tog, SKP, Nupp, K2, K2tog, YO, K3, Nupp, K2tog, SKP, K1, YO, SKP, K1, Nupp, K1, K2tog, YO, K3, YO, SKP, K1, Nupp, K1, K2tog, YO, K1, K2tog, K3, SI1.

Rows 6&8: P1, K4, P to 1 st before first B Marker, K1, P11, K1, P to last 5 sts, K4, P1.

Row 7: SI1, K3, SKP, K1, YO, SKP, K1, K2tog, YO, K5, YO, SKP, K1, K2tog, YO, K1, K2tog, K2, Nupp, K5, Nupp, K2, SKP, K1, YO, SKP, K1, K2tog, YO, K5, YO, SKP, K1, K2tog, YO, K1, K2tog, K3, SI1.

Row 9: SI1, K3, SKP, K1, YO, Sk2p, YO, K1, K2tog, YO, K1, YO, SKP, K1, YO, Sk2p, YO, K1, K2tog, SKP, K1, Nupp, K3, Nupp, K1, K2tog, SKP, K1, YO, Sk2p, YO, K1, K2tog, YO, K1, YO, SKP, K1, YO, Sk2p, YO, K1, K2tog, K3, SI1.

Rows 10 & 12: P1, K4, P to 1 st before first B Marker, K1, P9, K1, P to last 5 sts, K4, P1.

Row 11: SI1, K3, SKP, K3, K2tog, YO, K1, Nupp, K1, YO, SKP, K3, K2tog, K3, Nupp, K1, Nupp, K3, SKP, K3, K2tog, YO, K1, Nupp, K1, YO, SKP, K3, K2tog, K3, SI1.

Row 13: SI1, K3, SKP, K1, K2tog, YO, K1, Nupp, K1, Nupp, K1, YO, SKP, K1, K2tog, SKP, K2, Nupp, K2, K2tog, SKP, K1, K2tog, YO, K1, Nupp, K1, Nupp, K1, YO, SKP, K1, K2tog, K3, SI1.

Rows 14 & 16: P1, K4, P to 1 st before first B Marker, K1, P7, K1, P to last 5 sts, K4, P1.

Row 15: SI1, K3, SKP, K1, YO, SKP, K1, Nupp, K1, K2tog, YO, K1, K2tog, K7, SKP, K1, YO, SKP, K1, Nupp, K1, K2tog, YO, K1, K2tog, K3, SI1.

Row 17: SI1, K3, SKP, K1, YO, SKP, K1, K2tog, YO, K1, K2tog, SKP, K3, K2tog, SKP, K1, YO, SKP, K1, K2tog, YO, K1, K2tog, K3, SI1.

Rows 18 & 20: P1, K4, P to 1 st before first B Marker, K1, P5, K1, P to last 5 sts, K4, P1.

Row 19: SI1, K3, SKP, K1, YO, Sk2p, YO, K1, K2tog, K5, SKP, K1, YO, Sk2p, YO, K1, K2tog, K3, SI1.

Row 21: SI1, K3, SKP, K3, K2tog, SKP, K1, K2tog, SKP, K3, K2tog, K3, SI1.

Rows 22 & 24: P1, K to last st, P1.

Row 23: SI1, K3, SKP, K1, K2tog, Sk2p, SKP, K1, K2tog, K3, SI1

Row 25: SI1, K3, SKP, Sk2p, K2tog, K3, SI1

Row 26: P1, K9, P1 = 11 sts

DIRECTIONS

With larger needles cast on 623 sts using the Long Tail or Knitted CO Method.

Note: Temporarily placing a marker every 50 sts helps to keep track of the large number of sts as you CO.

Change to smaller needles and begin working Eos Setup Chart. Place Color A markers to mark beginning/end of each pattern repeat as indicated on the Setup Chart or at beginning/end of repeat indicated within brackets ( ) of the written pattern.

Work Chart One

Move/Add A Markers to beginning and end of repeats indicated with the red pattern box or indicated within brackets. A Markers are moved on Rows 9, 13 and 19. B Markers are placed on Row 9 which frame the Center Spine of the shawl. Center Spine sts are in bold. See chart for visual.

Work Chart Two

Remove A Markers for this chart. Move B Markers as indicated on chart with blue lines or as written in the instructions. Charted pattern repeat is repeated 69 times for checking stitch count.

Work Chart Three

Add A Markers to beginning and end of repeats indicated within the red pattern repeat box or as indicated within Row 1 brackets. Rows 1-10: Repeat pattern repeat in red box 15 times for each section.

Rows 11-16: Remove A Markers and place as shown by the red pattern repeat box. Repeat 8 times for each section.
Rows 17-28: Move/Add A Markers as shown by the red lines for the remaining Rows 17-28. Repeat between red lines 15 times for each section.

Work Chart Four

A Markers can be removed. Repeat pattern repeat 55 times to check stitch count.
B Markers remain to frame the Center Spine.

Work Chart Five: Sides and Chart Five: Center Spine

Work both charts at the same time. Read through the instructions for this section before beginning.

A Markers move on Row 1.

Work Side Chart Rows 1-12 once, then Rows 3-12 twelve times, then rows 3-4 once.

For the first repeat of the Sides Chart, repeat stitch pattern between the red solid lines 14 times for each side.

For the second repeat of the Sides Chart (Rows 3-12 only), there will be 1 repeat less per side (marked with red dash lines) or 13 repeats for each side.

In this way, each repeat of the Sides Chart Rows 3-12 will have 1 less repeat per side than the time before until all the repeats have been worked.

The Center Spine Section is worked between the two Side Chart sections. (See Chart for visual.)

Repeat Center Spine Rows 1-32 four times, then rows 1-12 once.

Work Chart Six

Any remaining A Markers can be removed on Row 1.

Finishing

Cut yarn and pull yarn through last st on needle leaving a 10" tail.

Pull the circular needle cable through the middle of the sts so that there are 6 sts on the front needle, RS facing you with needle tip pointing right. The back needle will have 5 sts, wrong sides together. Graft the sts together using Kitchener Stitch beginning with the first st on the back needle.

Weave in loose ends.

Block into shape as shown in schematic. Pull the tips down evenly adjusting from one side to the other .

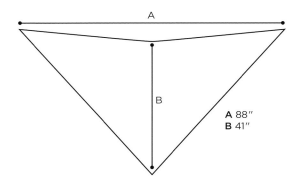

A 88"
B 41"

Set Up Chart

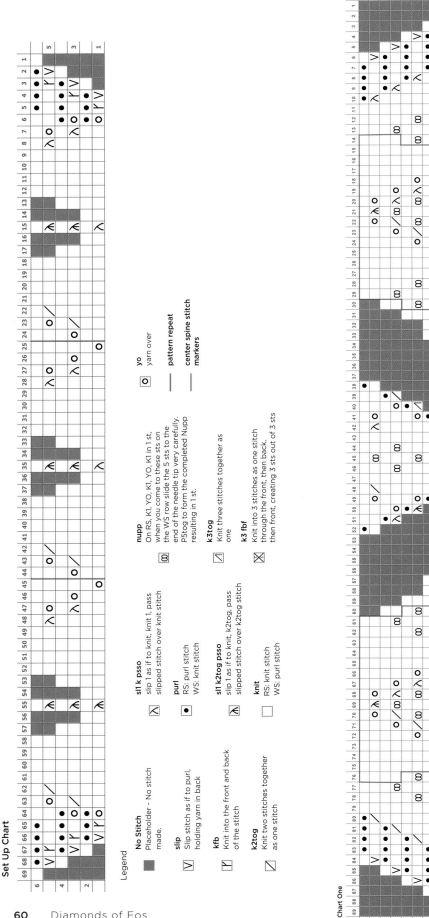

Chart One

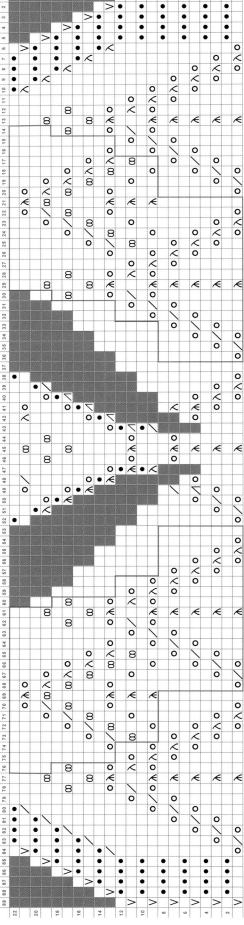

Legend

No Stitch
Placeholder - No stitch made.

slip
Slip stitch as if to purl, holding yarn in back

kfb
Knit into the front and back of the stitch

k2tog
Knit two stitches together as one stitch

sl1 k psso
slip 1 as if to knit, knit 1, pass slipped stitch over knit stitch

purl
RS: purl stitch
WS: knit stitch

sl1 k2tog psso
slip 1 as if to knit, k2tog, pass slipped stitch over k2tog stitch

knit
RS: knit stitch
WS: purl stitch

nupp
On RS, K1, YO, K1, YO, K1 in 1 st, when you come to these sts on the WS row slide the 5 sts to the end of the needle tip very carefully. P5tog to form the completed Nupp resulting in 1 st.

k3tog
Knit three stitches together as one

k3 fbf
Knit into 3 stitches as one stitch through the front, then back, then front, creating 3 sts out of 3 sts

yo
yarn over

pattern repeat

center spine stitch

markers

Chart Two

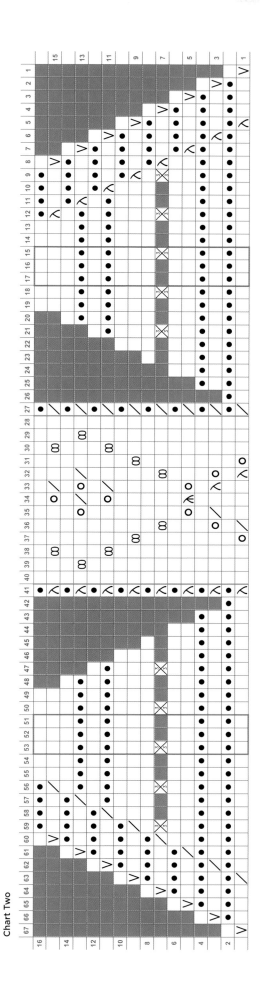

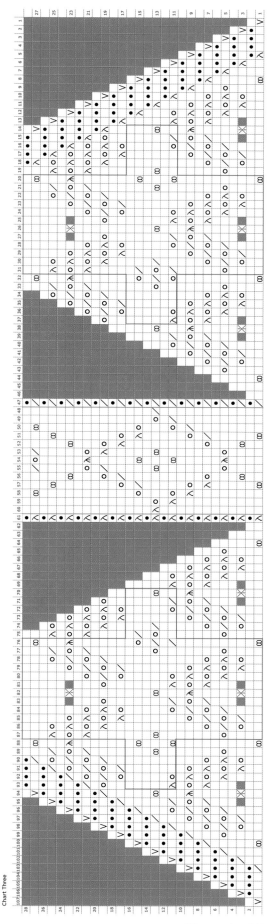

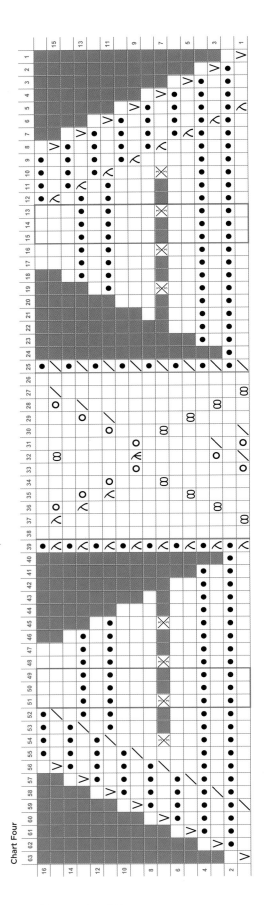

Chart Four

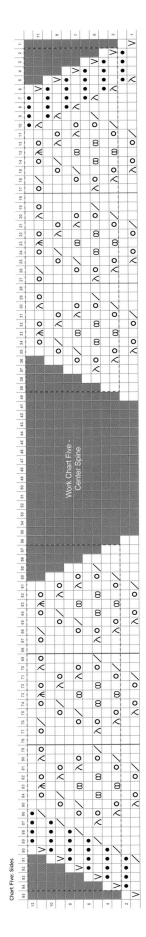

Chart Five: Sides

Work Chart Five - Center Spine

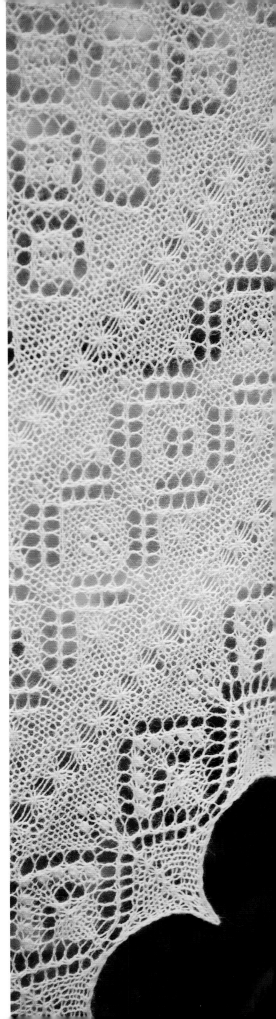

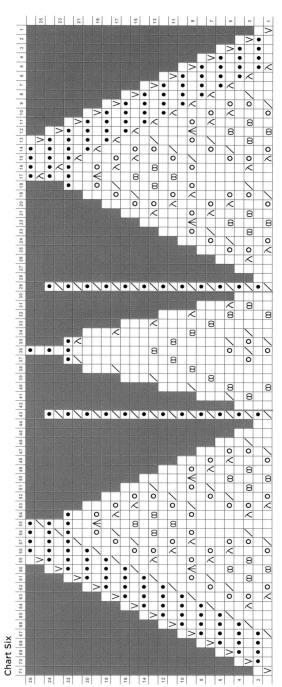

Chart Six

Chart Five - Center Spine

SWEET JALEBI

by Caroline Steinford

FINISHED MEASUREMENTS
19.25" wide x 73" long

YARN
Knit Picks Palette (100% Peruvian Highland Wool; 231 yards/50g): Mineral Heather 25546, 5 balls

NEEDLES
US 5 (3.75mm) straight or 24" circular needles or longer, or size to obtain gauge

NOTIONS
Yarn Needle
Stitch Markers

GAUGE
18 sts and 20 rows = 4" in St st, blocked.
21 sts and 22 rows = 4" over Webs Chart and Berry Stitch pattern, blocked

Sweet Jalebi

Notes:

Traditional Shetland patterns give elegant texture to a rectangular wrap based on dupattas worn in India. The designs along the edges of this stylish wrap mimic Jalebi, a festive East Indian funnel cake. Gauge is not critical, but changes may result in more yarn being needed. Since part of the design is actual knitted lace, with patterning on both sides, the design is suitable for experienced or adventurous knitters.

Read the charts RS rows (odd numbers) from right to left, and WS rows (even numbers) from left to right.

Webs Chart (worked flat over multiple of 18 sts)
Row 1 (RS): K7, K2tog, YO, K1, YO, SSK, K6.
Row 2 (WS): P1, P5, P2tog TBL, YO, P3, YO, P2tog, P6.
Row 3: K5, (K2tog, YO) twice, K1, (YO, SSK) twice, K4.
Row 4: P3, (P2tog TBL, YO) twice, P3, (YO, P2tog) twice, P4.
Row 5: K3, (K2tog, YO) 3 times, K1, (YO, SSK) 3 times, K2.
Row 6: P1, (P2tog TBL, YO) 3 times, P3, (YO, P2tog) 3 times, P2.
Row 7: K1, (K2tog, YO) 4 times, K1, (YO, SSK) 4 times.
Row 8: P1, (P2tog TBL, YO) 3 times, P3, (YO, P2tog) 3 times, P2.
Row 9: K3, (K2tog, YO) 3 times, K1, (YO, SSK) 3 times, K2.
Row 10: P3, (P2tog TBL, YO) twice, P3, (YO, P2tog) twice, P4.
Row 11: K5, (K2tog, YO) twice, K1, (YO, SSK) twice, K4.
Row 12: P5, P2tog TBL, YO, P3, YO, P2tog, P6.
Row 13: K7, K2tog, YO, K1, YO, SSK, K6.
Row 14: P7, YO, CDD, YO, P8.
Row 15: K7, YO, K2tog, K1, SSK, YO, K6.
Row 16: P5, YO, P2tog TBL, YO, CDD, YO, P2tog, YO, P6.
Row 17: K5, (YO, K2tog) twice, K1, (SSK, YO) twice, K4.
Row 18: P3, (YO, P2tog TBL) twice, YO, CDD, YO, (P2tog, YO) twice.
Row 19: K3, (YO, K2tog) 3 times, K1, (SSK, YO) 3 times, K2.
Row 20: P1, (YO, P2tog TBL) 3 times, YO, CDD, YO, (P2tog, YO) 3 times, P2.
Row 21: K3, (YO, K2tog) 3 times, K1, (SSK, YO) 3 times, K2.
Row 22: P3, (YO, P2tog TBL) twice, YO, CDD, YO, (P2tog, YO) twice, P4.
Row 23: K5, (YO, K2tog) twice, K1, (SSK, YO) twice, K4.
Row 24: P5, YO, P2tog TBL YO, CDD, YO, P2tog, YO, P6.
Row 25: K7, YO, K2tog, K1, SSK, YO, K6.
Row 26: P7, YO, CDD, YO, P8.
Rep Rows 1-26 for pattern.

Berry Stitch (worked flat over multiple of 4 sts)
Row 1 (RS): P.
Row 2 (WS): K3tog, (K1, P1, K1) into next st.
Row 3: P.
Row 4: (K1, P1, K1) into next st, K3tog.
Rep Rows 1-4 for pattern.

DIRECTIONS
CO 99 sts.

Garter Edge
K 3 rows.
Next Row: K4, PM, K91, PM, K4.

Wide Border
Row 1 (RS): K4, work Webs Chart 5 times across, K1, K4.
Row 2 (WS): K4, P1, work Webs Chart 5 times across, K4.
Work as established until Rows 1-26 of Webs Chart have been worked once.

Center Panel Bottom Border
Row 1 (RS): K4, work Webs Chart once, K1, PM, K53, PM, work Webs Chart once, K5.
Row 2 (WS): K4, P1, work Webs Chart once, K53, P1, work Webs Chart once, K4.
Row 3: K4, work Webs Chart once, K54, work Webs Chart once, K5.
Row 4: K4, P1, work Webs Chart once, K4, PM, K43, K2tog, PM, K4, P1, work Webs Chart once, K4. 1 st dec. 98 sts.

Center Panel
Row 1 (RS): K4, work Webs Chart once, K1, K4, work Berry Stitch chart to marker, K4, work Webs Chart once, K5.
Row 2 (WS): K4, P1, work Webs Chart once, K4, work Berry Stitch to marker, K4, P1, work Webs Chart once, K4.

Work as established until Rows 1-26 of Webs Chart have been worked 12 times total in this center section. Work Rows 1-22 once more, then begin Center Panel Top Border.

Center Panel Top Border
Row 1 (RS): K4, work Webs Chart once, K49, M1, K4, work Webs Chart once, K5. 1 st inc. 99 sts.
Rows 2 and 4 (WS): K4, P1, work Webs Chart once, K53, P1, work Webs Chart once, K4.
Row 3: K4, work Webs Chart once, K54, work Webs Chart once, K5.

Wide Border
Row 1 (RS): K4, work Webs Chart 5 times across, K5.
Row 2 (WS): K4, P1, work Webs Chart 5 times across, K4.

Work as established until Rows 1-26 of Webs Chart has been worked once.

Garter Edge
Remove all markers.

K 4 rows.

BO all sts.

Finishing
Weave in ends. Wash and block to finished measurements. Pin short edges to emphasize scallops between circles.

Webs Chart

Columns: 18 17 16 15 14 13 12 11 10 9 8 7 6 5 4 3 2 1

Rows (left side even): 26 24 22 20 18 16 14 12 10 8 6 4 2
Rows (right side odd): 25 23 21 19 17 15 13 11 9 7 5 3 1

Berry Stitch Chart

Columns: 4 3 2 1

Rows: 4, 3, 2, 1

Legend

purl
- ● RS: purl stitch
  WS: knit stitch

(k1 p1 k1) in 1 st
- Ⅴ RS: knit, purl and knit again all in the same st to make 3 sts from 1
  WS: purl, knit, and purl again all in the same stitch to make 3 sts from 1

No Stitch
- ■ Placeholder - No stitch made.

p3tog
- RS: Purl three stitches together as one
  WS: Knit three stitches together as one

k2tog
- RS: Knit two stitches together as one stitch
  WS: Purl 2 stitches together

□ **pattern repeat**

yo
- O yarn over

ssk
- RS: Slip one stitch as if to knit, Slip another stitch as if to knit. Insert left-hand needle into front of these 2 stitches and knit them together
  WS: Purl two stitches together in back loops, inserting needle from the left, behind and into the backs of the 2nd & 1st stitches in that order

Central Double Dec
- RS: Slip first and second stitches together as if to knit. Knit 1 stitch. Pass two slipped stitches over the knit stitch.
  WS: Slip first and second stitches together as it to purl through the back loop. Purl 1 stitch. Pass two slipped stitches over the purl stitch.

EMPERATRIZ SHAWL

by Danna Rachel Cauthern

FINISHED MEASUREMENTS

19.5" deep x 50" wingspan (Can be made larger with additional reps of Chart B.)

YARN

Knit Picks Gloss Lace (70% Merino Wool, 30% Silk; 440 yards/50g): Lilac 24846, 2 skeins.

NEEDLES

US 4 (3.5mm) 32 or longer circular needle, or size to obtain gauge

NOTIONS

Yarn Needle
Stitch Markers
525 Seed Beads Size 8/0 (optional)
Size 12 Steel Crochet Hook, or preferred beading tool (optional)

GAUGE

20 sts and 32 rows = 4" over Chart C lace patterns, blocked

Emperatriz Shawl

Notes:

Emperatriz (em-pe-ra-TREES) is a lace-weight shawl that combines traditional lace beauty with a contemporary crescent shape and optional beaded sparkle. It is 5/8 of a circle with a 3-stitch garter edge and 5 identical triangular wedges, each separated by a stitch. A single St st is used to frame each triangular wedge. The Lace Pattern is charted and is not too complicated – all wrong side rows are purled. The beads are optional and added as you go with a crochet hook or other beading tool to add a modern flair.

The shawl body is worked from 4 charts. Only the RS rows are shown on the charts and all WS chart rows are P. Read the chart RS rows from right to left. Rep pattern repeat sts in red brackets the appropriate number of times to complete the chart row. Take care to start each chart on the RS and end each chart after a WS row. Green sts indicate bead placement; beads should be added after st is worked.

Elastic Bind-off

K first 2 sts; *Sl these sts P-wise back to left hand needle, K these 2 sts tog TBL, K next st from left hand needle; rep from * to last 2 sts; K2tog TBL; cut yarn and pull through loop.

Beading with Crochet Hook

Work designated st. Place bead on crochet hook. Grab st loop on RH needle with hook facing you. Slide bead over top of hook onto st loop. Slide RH needle back through loop above the bead.

Centered Double Decrease (CDD)

Sl 2 sts together K-wise, K1, PSSO. 2 sts dec.

Sl-K2tog-PSSO (SK2P)

Sl 1, K2tog, PSSO. 2 sts dec.

DIRECTIONS

Garter Tab CO

CO 3 stitches. K 18 rows (9 garter ridges). PU and K9 sts, one at each garter ridge. PU and K3 sts from CO edge. 15 sts.

(The Garter Tab CO is not absolutely necessary. If desired, just CO 15 sts. You will have a little dip in your garter edge at the center with this method.)

Setup Rows

Row 1 (WS): K3, *PM, P1; rep from * 8 more times, PM, K3. 15 sts.
Row 2 (RS): K3, *SM, YO, K1, YO, SM, K1; rep from * 4 more times, K2. 25 sts. (This is Row 1 of Chart A.)
Row 3: K3, P to last marker, SM, K3.

Shawl Body

Next Row (RS): K3, *SM, work Chart A Row 3, SM, K1; rep from * 4 more times, K2.
Next Row (WS): K3, P to last marker, SM, K3.

Continue in pattern as established.

Work Chart A Rows 5-32 once. 95 sts.

Work Chart B Rows 1-24 twice. 215 sts. (For a larger shawl, work Chart B 4 times.)

Work Chart C Rows 1-60 once. 365 sts.

Work Chart D Rows 1-22 once. Sts marked in light green designate "points" for blocking. 425 sts.

Bind Off

With RS facing, BO all stitches using Stretchy BO.

Finishing

Weave in ends, wash and block aggressively to diagram or to desired shape and size. Use sts marked in light green and the sts that separate each shawl wedge as points for blocking.

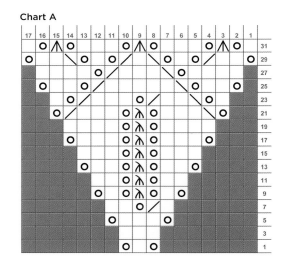

Chart A

Legend

▪	**No Stitch** Placeholder - No stitch made.	▫	**pattern repeat**
⊙	**yo** yarn over	▪	**bead**
▫	**knit** knit stitch	▪	**blocking point**
╱	**k2tog** Knit two stitches together as one stitch		
⋏	**sk2p** slip 1, k2tog, pass slip stitch over k2tog		
╲	**ssk** Slip one stitch as if to knit, slip another stitch as if to knit. Insert left-hand needle into front of these 2 stitches and knit them together		
⋀	**Central Double Dec** Slip first and second stitches together as if to knit. Knit 1 stitch. Pass two slipped stitches over the knit stitch.		

Chart B

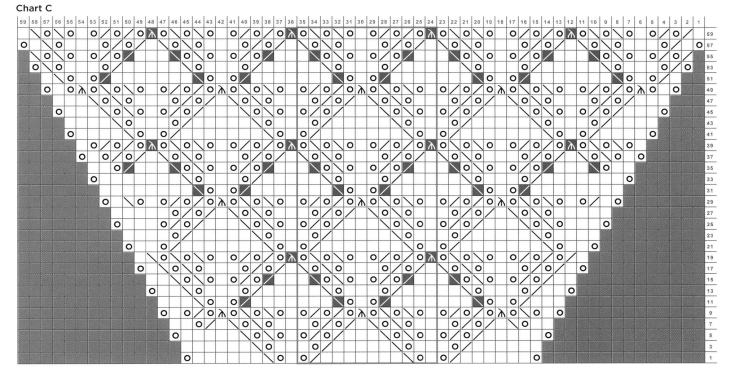

Chart C

Chart D

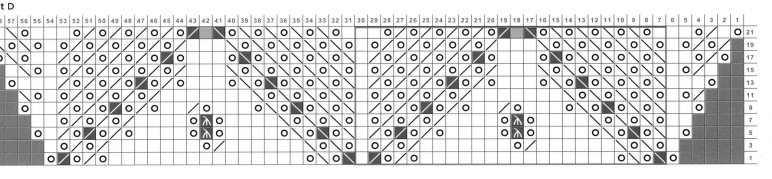

CASCADIAN STOLE

by Nikki Wagner

FINISHED MEASUREMENTS
22.25" x 64"

YARN
Knit Picks Alpaca Cloud Lace (100% Baby Alpaca; 440 yards/50g): Diana 26762, 4 skeins

NEEDLES
US 1 (2.25 mm) straight or circular needles, or size to obtain gauge

NOTIONS
Yarn Needle
Stitch Markers
Blocking Pins

GAUGE
24 sts and 64 rows = 4" over Chevron Lace pattern, blocked.
24 sts and 56 rows = 4" over Diamond Lace pattern, blocked.
24 sts and 56 rows = 4" over Stockinette stitch, blocked

Cascadian Stole

Notes:

The I-Cord Edge pattern is worked at the beginning of every row, with the exception of the CO and BO rows. The Chevron Lace and Diamond Lace patterns are both charted. Only the Chevron Lace pattern is written. The charted and written lace patterns are repeated between the stitch markers.

Center Double Decrease (CDD): Sl 2 sts together K-wise, K1, pass 2 Sl sts over the st just knit.

Double Yarn Over (YO2x): Bring the yarn forward, wrap yarn around the right-hand needle (from front to back) twice before proceeding to work the next st as instructed.
On the rows following the YO2x, P into the first YO and K into the second YO.

Read the charts RS rows (odd numbers) from right to left.

I-Cord Edge (worked over 3 sts at each end of row)
RS Row: WYIB, Sl 3 sts K-wise, work as instructed to last 3 sts, K3.
WS Row: WYIF, Sl 3 sts P-wise, work to last 3 sts as instructed, P3.
Rep these two rows for pattern.

Chevron Lace (worked flat over multiple of 8 sts)
Row 1: SSK, (K1, YO) twice, K1, K2tog, K1.
Row 2 (and all even rows): P.
Row 3: Rep Row 1.
Row 5: YO, SSK, K3, K2tog, YO, K1.
Row 7: K1, YO, SSK, K1, K2tog, YO, K2.
Row 9: K2, YO, CDD, YO, K3.
Row 10: P.
Rep Rows 1-10 for pattern.

Diamond Lace (worked flat over multiple of 62 sts)
All Even Rows (WS): P across, working P1, K1 in the YO2x sts from the previous row. No st increases made.
Repeat Rows 1-116 for pattern.

Yarn Over BO
K1, *YO, K1, use left needle to lift YO and first K1 over last K1 and off of right needle; rep from * until 1 st remains. Break yarn and pull through remaining st.

DIRECTIONS

Stole
The stole begins and ends with the Chevron Lace pattern and the middle section is worked in the Diamond Lace pattern.

Loosely CO 136 sts.

Chevron Lace Edge
Set up Row (WS): WYIF, Sl 3 sts P-wise, P1, PM, P to last 4 sts, PM, P4.
Row 1 (RS): WYIB, Sl 3 sts K-wise, K1, SM, work Chevron Lace pattern to next marker, SM, K4.
Row 2 (WS): WYIF, Sl 3 sts P-wise, P to end.

Continue in pattern as established, working I-Cord Edge at each side and working the Chevron Lace Pattern between st markers.

Rep Rows 1-10 of the Chevron Lace Pattern 4 times total. Remove markers on last row.

Next Row: Work I-Cord Edge, work in St st to last 3 sts, work I-Cord Edge.
Repeat last row 6 more times, ending with a RS row.

Diamond Lace Body
Set up Row (WS): WYIF, Sl 3 sts P-wise, P3, PM, P to last 6 sts, PM, P6.
Row 1 (RS): WYIB, Sl 3 sts K-wise, K3, SM, work Diamond Lace pattern to next marker, SM, K6.
Row 2 (WS): WYIF, Sl 3 sts P-wise, P3, SM, work Diamond Lace pattern to next marker, SM, P6.

Work Rows 1-116 of the Diamond Lace pattern 7 times total. Remove markers on last row.

Next Row: Work I-Cord Edge, work in St st to last 3 sts, work I-Cord Edge.

Repeat last row 7 more times.

Repeat instructions for Chevron Lace edge.

BO on RS using the Yarn Over BO method.

Finishing
Weave in ends, wash and block to diagram. Block the lace edges so that they are straight along the edge. Pin the I-Cord edges to measurements.

Diamond Lace Chart

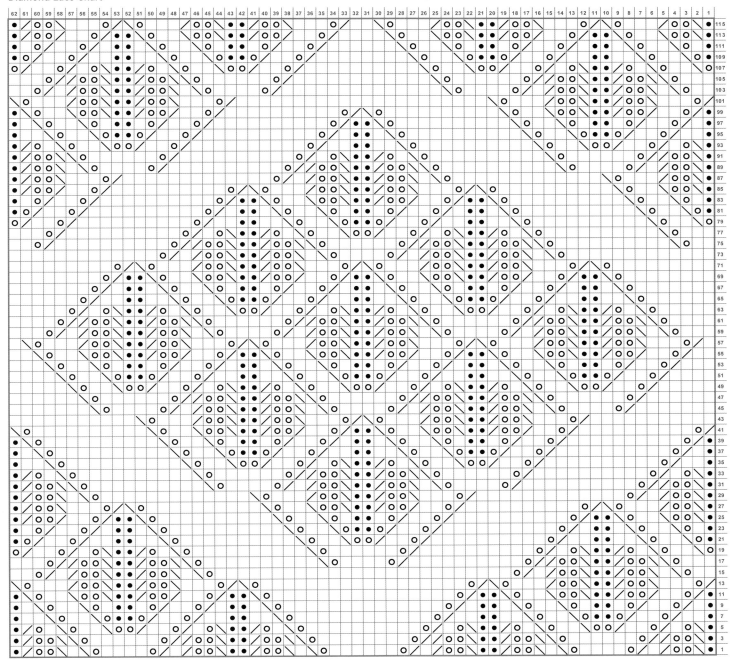

Chevron Lace Chart

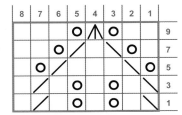

Legend

ssk
Slip one stitch as if to knit, slip another stitch as if to knit. Insert left-hand needle into front of these 2 stitches and knit them together

knit
knit stitch

yo
Yarn over

k2tog
Knit two stitches together as one stitch

Central Double Dec
Slip first and second stitches together as if to knit. Knit 1 stitch. Pass two slipped stitches over the knit stitch

pattern repeat

IN PERFECT HARMONY

by Cally Monster

FINISHED MEASUREMENTS
68" wingspan x 24" deep

YARN
Luminance (100% Silk; 439 yards/50g):
Zen 27054, 2 skeins

NEEDLES
US 4 (3.5mm) circular needles, or size to
obtain gauge
US 6 (4mm) circular needles, or 2 sizes
larger than size to obtain gauge

NOTIONS
Yarn Needle
Stitch Markers (optional)
Blocking Wires and T-pins

GAUGE
24 sts and 32 rows= 4" in St st with
smaller needles, or size to obtain gauge,
blocked.
The following chart gauges are with
smaller needles, aggressively blocked, or
size to obtain gauge.
18 sts and 26 rows = 4" over lace Chart A.
18 sts and 28 rows = 4" across the middle
of Chart B.
Correct gauge is not critical for this
project, but your final measurements and
yardage requirements may vary if your
gauge is different

In Perfect Harmony

Notes:

In Perfect Harmony is a top down crescent shaped shawl with an elegant border. Designed from a variety of traditional lace patterns, In Perfect Harmony transforms old world lace into an elegant modern heirloom. This crescent shaped shawl has been designed to be knit in lace weight yarn giving you a fine and airy lace effect. The shape helps it stay on your shoulders, wrapping you up in delicate beauty. The 3-stitch garter stitch edging frames the intricate lace patterns, then sweeps into a timeless edge. You'll find this pattern to be for advanced knitters.

These charts are designed so that a given symbol represents the same exact stitch on the RS and the WS (i.e. an open box mean "knit" on both the RS and the WS). Read the charts RS rows (odd numbers) from right to left, and WS rows (even numbers) from left to right.

Shawl is worked back and forth from the top down. A circular needle is used to accommodate the large number of stitches.

If using stitch markers between repeats, note that the stitch markers will move on Chart C, starting with Row 21 through end of chart, Chart E, starting Row 21 and continuing through Chart F.

DIRECTIONS

Using smaller needles, CO 4 sts. You may want to place a removable stitch marker in each CO loop to show where you'll be picking up stitches later.

K 13 rows.

After last row, do not turn work, PU and K6 sts along the edge of the small garter stitch rectangle, PU and K4 sts from CO loops. 14 sts.

Shawl Body

Work Chart A Rows 1-38 once, working repeat 3 times across. 103 sts.

Work Chart B Rows 1-26 once, working repeat 7 times across. 168 sts.

Work Chart C Rows 1-40 once, working repeat 8 times across. 274 sts.

Work Chart D Rows 1-14 once, working repeat 52 times across. 302 sts.

Switch to larger needles.
Work Chart E Rows 1-24 once, working repeat 13 times across. 585 sts.

Work Chart F Rows 1-18 once, working repeat 13 times across. 460 sts.

BO loosely K-wise.

Finishing

Weave in ends.

Block aggressively to dimensions as follows, thread flexible wires or T-pins through the eyelet row and pin in a crescent shape, then pin out each of the yarn overs on the edge between each flower stem into crescent shapes.

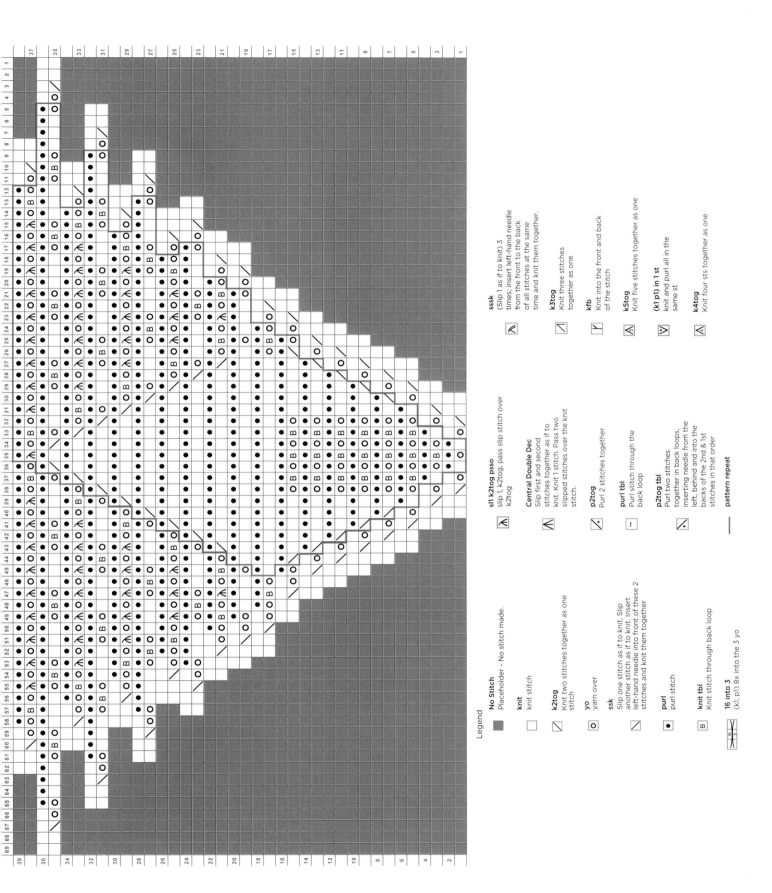

Legend

No Stitch
Placeholder - No stitch made.

knit
knit stitch

| / | k2tog
Knit two stitches together as one stitch |
| O | yo
yarn over |
| / | ssk
Slip one stitch as if to knit. Slip another stitch as if to knit. Insert left-hand needle into front of these 2 stitches and knit them together |
| • | purl
purl stitch |
| B | knit tbl
Knit stitch through back loop |
| | 16 into 3
(K1, p1) 8x into the 3 yo |

| ⋀ | s1 k2tog psso
slip 1, K2tog, pass slip stitch over k2tog |
| ⋀ | Central Double Dec
Slip first and second stitches together as if to knit. Knit 1 stitch. Pass two slipped stitches over the knit stitch. |
| \ | p2tog
Purl 2 stitches together |
| ᴙ | purl tbl
Purl stitch through the back loop |
| ⋰ | p2tog tbl
Purl two stitches together in back loops, inserting needle from the left, behind and into the backs of the 2nd & 1st stitches in that order |
| — | pattern repeat |

| | sssk
(Slip 1 as if to knit) 3 times; insert left-hand needle from the front to the back of all stitches at the same time and knit them together. |
| ⋏ | k3tog
Knit three stitches together as one |
| Y | kfb
Knit into the front and back of the stitch |
| ⋀ | k5tog
Knit five stitches together as one |
| ∨ | (k1 p1) in 1 st
knit and purl all in the same st |
| ⋀ | k4tog
Knit four sts together as one |

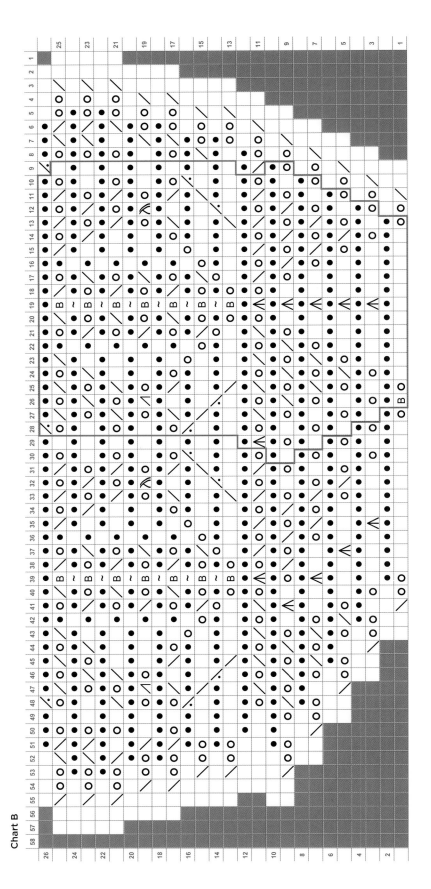

Chart C

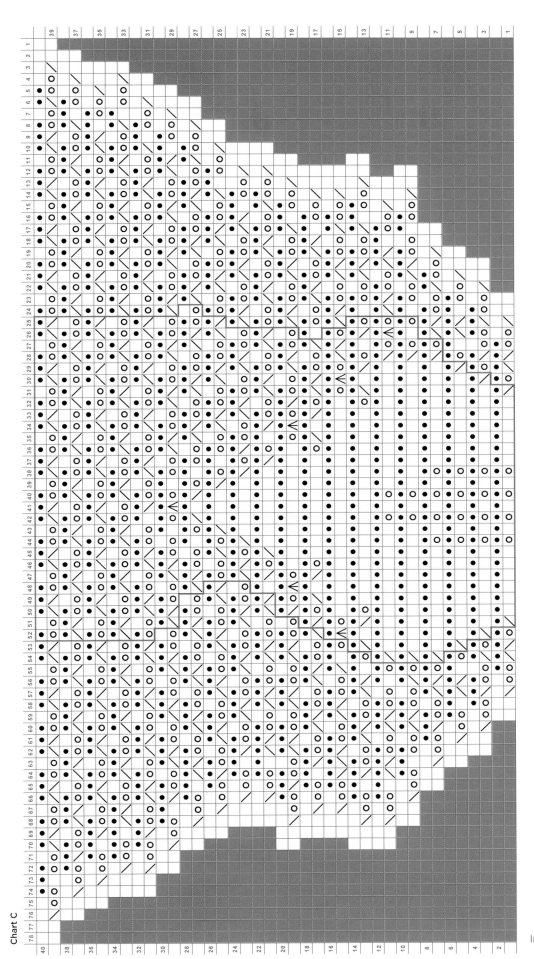

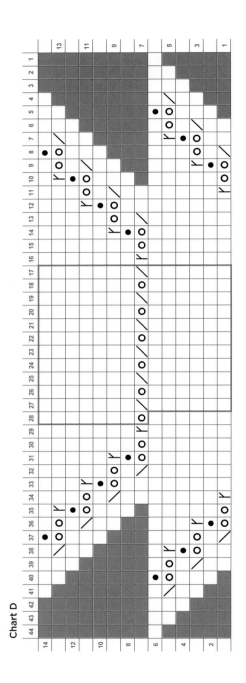

Chart D

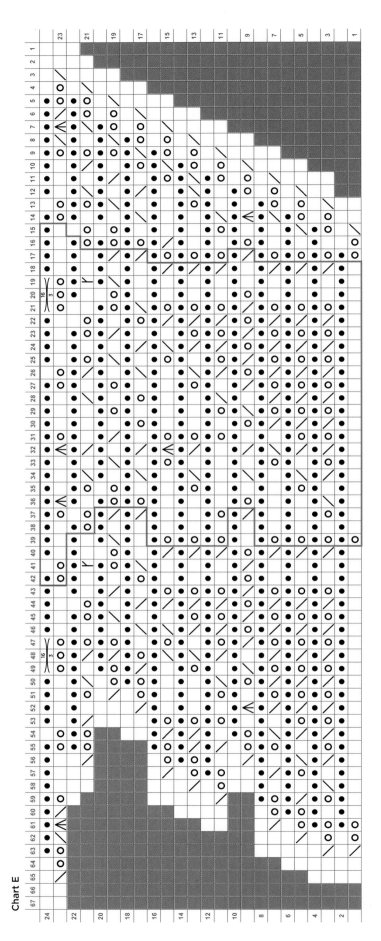

Chart E

Chart F

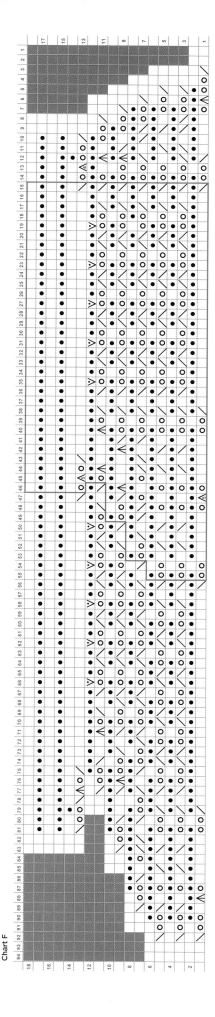

ROSEWOOD STOLE

by Kalurah Hudson

FINISHED MEASUREMENTS
15" x 110" not including picots, blocked

YARN
Knit Picks Alpaca Cloud Fingering (100% Superfine Alpaca; 200 yards/50g): Rebecca 26893, 5 hanks

NEEDLES
US 4 (3.50mm) straight or circular needles, or size to obtain gauge

NOTIONS
Yarn Needle
Stitch Markers
T-pins and lace wires for blocking

GAUGE
3 Diamond Lace Chart repeats = 15" x 5", blocked

Rosewood Stole

Notes:

An elegant diamond lace pattern is showcased in this oversized stole. The edging is knit at the same time as the stole stitches and a picot trim highlights the ends. Alpaca lends warmth and softness, while keeping this a lightweight wrap with incredible drape.

Cable CO

Insert RH needle between 2 sts on LH needle, front to back, YO needle and pull a loop through to the front, place the loop onto the end of the LH needle K-wise. 1 st CO.

Picot CO

CO 4, turn work, BO 2, *place stitch back onto LH needle P-wise, Cable CO 4, BO 2; rep from * until you reach desired number of CO sts.

Picot BO

Cable CO 2, BO 4, *place stitch back onto LH needle P-wise, Cable CO 2, BO 4; rep from * until all sts are BO.

Read the charts RS rows (odd numbers) from right to left and WS rows (even numbers) from left to right.

DIRECTIONS

Work Picot CO until there are 62 sts on needle. 31 picots.

K 1 row.

Work Rows 1-12 of Chart 66 times, or until piece measures approximately 110" from CO edge, not including picots.

K 1 row.

Work Picot BO on RS. 30 picots.

Finishing

Weave in ends, spray block to finished dimensions.

Rosewood Chart

(Chart columns numbered 62 to 1, rows 1–12. Lace pattern worked in knit, purl, yarn over, k2tog, central double dec, and ssk stitches.)

Legend

knit
RS: knit stitch
WS: purl stitch

purl
RS: purl stitch
WS: knit stitch

No Stitch
Placeholder – No stitch made.

yo
yarn over

k2tog
RS: Knit two stitches together as one stitch
WS: Purl 2 stitches together

Central Double Dec
RS: Slip first and second stitches together as if to knit. Knit 1 stitch. Pass two slipped stitches over the knit stitch.
WS: Slip first and second stitches together as it to purl through the back loop. Purl 1 stitch. Pass two slipped stitches over the purl stitch.

ssk
RS: Slip one stitch as if to knit, Slip another stitch as if to knit. Insert left-hand needle into front of these 2 stitches and knit them together
WS: Purl two stitches together in back loops, inserting needle from the left, behind and into the backs of the 2nd & 1st stitches in that order

Abbreviations			M	marker			stitch		TBL	through back loop
BO	bind off		M1	make one stitch		RH	right hand		TFL	through front loop
cn	cable needle		M1L	make one left-leaning		rnd(s)	round(s)		tog	together
CC	contrast color			stitch		RS	right side		W&T	wrap & turn (see
CDD	Centered double dec		M1R	make one right-lean-		Sk	skip			specific instructions
CO	cast on			ing stitch		Sk2p	sl 1, k2tog, pass			in pattern)
cont	continue		MC	main color			slipped stitch over		WE	work even
dec	decrease(es)		P	purl			k2tog: 2 sts dec		WS	wrong side
DPN(s)	double pointed		P2tog	purl 2 sts together		SKP	sl, k, psso: 1 st dec		WYIB	with yarn in back
	needle(s)		PM	place marker		SL	slip		WYIF	with yarn in front
EOR	every other row		PFB	purl into the front and		SM	slip marker		YO	yarn over
inc	increase			back of stitch		SSK	sl, sl, k these 2 sts tog			
K	knit		PSSO	pass slipped stitch		SSP	sl, sl, p these 2 sts tog			
K2tog	knit two sts together			over			tbl			
KFB	knit into the front and		PU	pick up		SSSK	sl, sl, sl, k these 3 sts			
	back of stitch		P-wise	purlwise			tog			
K-wise	knitwise		rep	repeat		St st	stockinette stitch			
LH	left hand		Rev St st	reverse stockinette		sts	stitch(es)			

Knit Picks yarn is both luxe and affordable—a seeming contradiction trounced! But it's not just about the pretty colors; we also care deeply about fiber quality and fair labor practices, leaving you with a gorgeously reliable product you'll turn to time and time again.

THIS COLLECTION FEATURES

Palette
Fingering Weight
100% Peruvian Highland Wool

Luminance
Lace Weight
100% Silk

Alpaca Cloud Lace
Lace Weight
100% Baby Alpaca

Shimmer
Fingering Weight
70% Baby Alpaca, 30% Silk

Capretta
Fingering Weight
80% Fine Merino Wool, 10% Cashmere, 10% Nylon

Shadow
Lace Weight
100% Merino Wool

Gloss Lace
Lace Weight
70% Merino Wool, 30% Silk

Alpaca Cloud Fingering
Fingering Weight
100% Superfine Alpaca

View these beautiful yarns and more at www.KnitPicks.com